Celebrate HER Now!

An Interactive Guide to Loving Ourselves
And Embracing Female Youth
of the Hip-Hop Generation

By

Lacey C. Clark!

Lacey C. Clark!

The contents of this book are merely for the purposes of education and information. This book is not intended to be a substitute for therapy or professional advice.

Celebrate HER Now!

Lacey C. Clark!

Published by: Sisters' Sanctuary

This book contains certain media elements copyrighted by Microsoft and used according to the End-User License Agreement for Microsoft Software.

Copyright © 2006 by Lacey C. Clark
ISBN: **978-1-4116-8591-8**

First Edition, 2006
Published in the United States of America

Cover Design: Gary Carr
Illustrations: Lacey C. Clark!

Lacey C. Clark!

Dedication

To the woman who sees little Danisha on the street corner, thong showing and breasts out, and shakes her head in dismay. To you, who want to do something, but don't know what, how, when, or where.

To the young sister around the way who does not know that she is beautiful, powerful and remarkable *way* beyond her exterior. She deserves to be celebrated! She deserves to know that she is AWESOME!!

Lacey C. Clark!

This workbook/journal is designed for mothers, mentors and aspiring role models to address the emotional needs of our female youth. The "HER" in Celebrate HER Now! is defined as female youth.
The mission is to inspire our youth to be greater than we are for the future of humanity.

Contents

MISSION I

I LOVE MYSELF BECAUSE . . .

MISSION II

I EMBRACE OUR FEMALE YOUTH BY:

Lacey C. Clark!

SISTERS' SANCTUARY ANTHEM
By Elisha R. Jennings

Right now...I'm just good,
but GREAT is seeping through my seams
The next level is waiting and I must climb
to reach my dreams
Gotta be strong to shake the snakes, the fakes
and the ones who say I don't have what it takes
huh...while they're hatin', I'm creatin'...

MY VERY OWN SANCTUARY

A sacred place where I come face to face with me - the
ONLY one who can keep me from being free
Alternating sessions of meditation, conversation and relaxation
In **MY SANCTUARY**, there's an on-going celebration of
my outer **and** inner elevation
Truth, Respect, Honor and Positivity are all extended an
invitation in the form of
Thought
I think them, and so they come
Bringing with them Wellness, Self-Acceptance, Self-Love and
that hard to reach one ...Peace
The release that every sister in the Universe seeks

This here **SISTERS' SANCTUARY** is empowering
My own portable ladder that keeps me towering over foes and
sitting right under the nose of
Spirit
Height muting idle chatter...I'm so high I can't even hear it
Rose petals flutter from my every breath
Excuses born out of mediocrity drop to their death
It's about that A+, I'm layin' the F to rest, and yes
Life **is** one hell of a test

But in **MY SANCTUARY**, I can explore and find answers
I no longer have to guess
I no longer feel stressed and oppressed
I'm crackin' the whole damn thing open…UNBLOCKED,
UNBOUND and UNCHAINED
I'm totally free to express
cause **MY SANCTUARY** keeps me blessed

The Divine spirits of the sisters before me can rest
Those original architects who laid the blueprint for the rest
The sisterly in me won't let me forget
the sisters here and after me who still have yet
to begin to build
or understand that any mission they attempt will remain
unfulfilled
until self-hate is killed
It's all about unleashing the beauty within them
and that's real

So here's the deal…
I say we all come together, put it all on the table
and work it all out until all of us are able
to be a holistic homeowner
The materials are abundant cause the Universe is a gracious
donor

A **SISTERS' SANCTUARY** is a place where a sister can go to
grow and know
that everything is in Divine Order
that she carries within her the light and the water she needs to
blossom
her sanctuary is the soil that nourishes and empowers
For she is a flower

Introduction

When you think of the number 13, what comes to mind? Is it the scary movie Friday the 13th? Perhaps you think of it as an omen.

The first calendar to record time was the Lunar calendar, a timetable that measures the phases of the moon and consists of 28 days per month (with one additional day). What else occurs every 28 days? If you said your menstrual cycle, you guessed correctly! Our bodies were the first system of measurement of when time began. 365/28 = 13; there are 13 months in a lunar year.

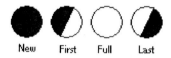

New   First   Full   Last

Because of the parallels between menstrual cycles and moon phases, women were believed to have known how to predict the seasons of the year, the migrations of animals such as birds and fish, and how to forecast childbirth with the accuracy of a day.[1] Our ancient culture, which originated in Egypt, was matriarchal and, matrilineal; it was based on astrology and cosmology.

In their efforts to destroy the ancient maternal kinship groupings and their sacred ways of existing, Christian missionaries robbed people of their land, stole the earth's natural resources, and exploited human labor while introducing the concept of a Father God (the antithesis of Mother Earth) who was the enemy of matrifocal societies.

European patriarchy professes everything female is the root of all evil. Recall of the story of Adam and Eve: it was Eve who was disobedient in the Garden of Eden, and thus punished by menstruation and painful childbirth.

"Patriarchy divides life into higher and lower categories, such as 'spirit' versus nature' or 'mind versus matter,' and typically in this alienated symbolism, the superior 'spirit/mind' is male and/or white, while the inferior 'nature/matter' is female and/or black."[2] Judaism, Christianity, Islam, and other religions established under patriarchal order say that the sins of man began with the disobedience of woman. Menstruation is considered a punishment rather than a life-giving gift; a bestowal that has laid the foundation for measurements of time, mathematics, and agriculture. The detachment from this ancient science and the implementation of the white European patriarchal rule established in the early centuries was the creation of misogyny.

Could this way of thinking be the deep-seeded cause of and justification for the physical, mental, emotional, financial and spiritual abuse of women? Could this be the subconscious rationalization for rape, exploitation and dehumanization?

Let us go on a brief historical journey.

Until the mid 1800's, white women were regarded as the property of their husbands and black women as the property of her white master first, and her Black husband second. The Black husband nor the wife had any rights as a slave. Black women were raped, even gang raped, and tortured, often with no legal recourse for her attackers. Black women had few civil rights, were still civilly dead well into the 20th century. Rape reported by a Black woman was not taken seriously when reported to authorities. From being forced to open her legs for the "Massa," to being forced to deliver a baby from an unwanted sexual experience, to being a wet nurse and caretaker/nanny to the master's children, putting their needs above her own children's, her Black body did not belong to her.

Even her children were stripped from her and sold to other plantations. Article IX of the Christian Black Codes of 1724 states that children born from slaves shall become property of their mother's master. In every way, we as Black women have been stripped of our culture, identity, and humanity. We have been treated as everything but the spiritual human beings we are, hence our sexuality has been bruised and has become unhealthy.

I wrote this interactive book because our communities are in a crisis.

"What can I say? My butt is my identity. It makes me who I am and it is a big part of me. My mom says it looks like two big ole hams in my pants."

-Absolute Amber

"Bottom's Up", *King Magazine,* July-August 2005

"I am mad at myself because I have two kids by the same father. I gotta get rid of my kids' father because I need me a new daddy 'cuz my kids ain't supposed to have the same dad."

- Girl, Age 16 (2005)

Our youths are in a state of emergency. The time for action is now!

According to the Centers for Disease Control and Prevention (CDC), although African-Americans represent only 12.3 percent of the U.S. population, we account for more than half of all new HIV infections annually, more than any other racial or ethnic population. In addition, while HIV/AIDS was the leading cause of death for African-Americans between the ages

25 to 44 during the year 2000, it was only the fifth leading cause of death for whites.

Furthermore, according to the World Health Organization (WHO), Black women account for the increasing numbers of new HIV cases in the United States, and AIDS is now the leading cause of death for U.S. Black women between the ages of 25 to 32.

Music videos that turn women into objects for sexual domination are becoming soft-core pornography that our children consume regularly. A verse from famous rapper Notorious B.I.G. states "money, clothes, and hoes - all a nigga knows."[3] Although never fully respected, we as Black women are disgraced worldwide through the sexual images projected on television for the **entire world to see!!** We are failing our children, the Hip-Hop generation. We no longer have the option to just focus on ourselves and just mind our own business. We are all responsible.

Little John, Ludacris, and 50 Cent are doing what all of us are doing to survive in a capitalist society: working and meeting the demands of our careers. However, these music artists are chart toppers because they meet the demand for rap lyrics that have women *"bending over to the front, and touching their toes."[4]* At some point if we gave this matter any serious thought, we would cringe and be offended by these lyrics. Yet some of us have become so de-sensitized to being disrespected, dehumanized, and **carnalized** that we end up merely tapping our feet, snapping our fingers, and celebrating our own demise.

But it is not just the music and videos.

We are a people in pain. Consciously and subconsciously affected by the remnants of slavery, we self-medicate with our many addictions, one being consumerism. We believe that if we purchase a powerful, sexy, or expensive outfit by *Gucci* or *Louis Vuitton*, or wear all white or symbols of ankhs, we can convince the world that we are **okay**. We try our best to be homogenous to compete with European Americans, but they do not share the effects of our history in America. We can choose to ignore how we are viewed, but our perceived lack of value in this country and worldwide will always prevail if we do nothing. This has been shown by our portrayal in the news media, going all the way back to Saarjite Baartman, a young Khosian woman from Southern Africa whose nude body was the main attraction at public spectacles (circus) in both England and France (Early 1800's). From the original Colt 45 advertisements featuring scantily-clad women, to today's music video-pornography.

Additionally, we do not value ourselves enough in our relationships. Often, we sacrifice our own well-being, safety, and peace of mind to save and protect our abuser, even after we have been beaten, raped, verbally abused, infected with an STD, stolen from and cheated on. But what about *you*? Will you become a **statistic?**

Celebrate HER Now! is an interactive and practical guide that will teach you how to put yourself first, while celebrating both your inner-youth and adulthood. Its mission is to help you examine the many layers of what makes you unique and acknowledge those characteristics about yourself that you dislike. The larger mission is to alter the course of this generation so that our grandchildren, great-grandchildren, and great-greats can know what it is to be human, healed, and whole. The madness of this world must end and it begins with *you*!

When you choose to help yourself, you set an example for our daughters. Influence the world with your greatness. Remind our men to be respectful, and rear our sons to understand the depth and beauty of our sacredness and value.

Lacey C. Clark!

Tight Jean Skirt: Lacey's Testimony

September, 2002

*"Oh, Oh, Oh, they want to fuck HER,
they want to rub their dicks on her precious clitoris,
watch them big ol' titties settle and part a bit."[5]*

-The Thickness
Jill Scott Experience :Jill Scott, 2001

"Oh my God!" I thought, "Jill Scott's talking about me."

Flashback: *July, 1991*

Tight jean skirt. White tee. Summer. I sat on a fire hydrant on a street corner in North Philadelphia. I made sure to push my buttocks over the top of the hydrant so that anyone who walked past or drove by could see a meaty mass before them.

Tanel and I walked what now seems like the four corners of our neighborhood… to get noticed, beeped at…*carnally* stared at.

This was the only way I felt good. I ate a bag of Bar-B-Q potato chips, my favorite.

As I sat on the hydrant and waited for Tanel to purchase *HER* stuff on what would be our fifth trip to the corner store, Kajim, the cutest boy up 31st Street walked by and grabbed my 12-year-old ass. He may have been 18 or 19. He didn't care how old I was and neither did I.

19

Lacey C. Clark!

"Oh my GOD!" I thought, "Kajim likes me." With no acknowledgement of my face or name, he caressed my ass like he owned it, like it belonged to him. And deep inside I wanted it to. Shit, Kajim was cute.

Tanel finally came out of the store. I think she bought a red *Hug*. I celebrated, "Ooooh girl, guess who touched my butt?!"

We laughed as we excitedly left the corner. I was happy that day, felt good about myself. Kajim was like the 31st Street legend. He could get any girl he wanted, so for him to touch my butt must have meant I was cute, sexy, attractive, especially because I was dark-skinned, and all the desirable girls were light.

I thought about the endless times I went to bed praying to have light skin, long hair and fingernails like Rita, the Puerto Rican girl down my grandma's way. I was pudgy, dark-skinned, and my hair never really flowed in the wind. It was important for me to be liked, wanted, especially since Kajim's girlfriend looked like Rita. His touching my butt meant I was beautiful.

I missed my dad. I think he was in jail at the time. Before he left, Dee (my dad's girlfriend), my dad, Poppy and me would hang out down South Street in the springtime. Dad would notice the men looking at my developing body. "You see... you see them looking at *HER*?" Dee would tell me how he would nudge her in concern. Dee and I would laugh. My dad never said anything to me. I guess he just didn't know how. Maybe he was too embarrassed to tell me what men really thought.

At 33rd Street, I stood waiting for the bus to go to Creative and Performing Arts (CAPA), my high school. That morning I wanted to be cute: knee length boots, above the knee skirt, short locks. Nobody rocked locks in Philly in 1995. I wore them because it celebrated my Blackness, but what about my developing womanhood?

20

On that beautiful spring morning, I dressed to impress. 33rd Street was like a mini-highway with a traffic light at my bus stop. "Wassup big legs, mustache... um, you *must* have a hairy pussy," the men would say to me on their way to work, honking their horns, some probably married with kids, others old enough to have grandkids. My bus came, and I got on. While something inside me felt good, another side didn't understand what was wrong. I was 16. Was there another way?

...Put it in my mouth
She said put it in her mouth
I said my muthaf**in mouth, I mean her muthaf**in mouth
Put it in my mouth ...[6]

I liked that song "Put it in Your Mouth" by Akinyele. I would chant it at the house parties around my way as a means of rebellion. Although I never did all the things the song listed, perhaps because of an imaginary boundary my mother helped me to create, I later learned that so many of my friends had put "it" in places that weren't comfortable, seeking love, attention, and validation.

Some of them started at age four or maybe sooner, against their will and didn't know how to stop. They just didn't know any other way. Girlhood innocence stolen, lost, called to and pushed out the window; shattered pieces of their humanity. Where is their haven? Who tells them, who tell *us*, that we are worth more?

Flash Forward: ***November, 2002***

"Yooooo, Phat Ass!" A group of teen girls all wearing waist length jackets and form fitting jeans, some with thongs exposed, look at each other indecisively.

"The one in the Blue Jacket!" The one in the blue jacket slows her walk.

21

As "Blue Jacket" falls behind, two men seeming to be in their twenties with oversized jeans and Timberland boots waddle over to *HER*. The shorter of the two males makes his way to the group of girls now waiting for their friend.

"BJ" and the taller male exchange words. I can't hear what they are saying but I see that he's all in her face. He turns *HER* around sure to let *HER* know how "phat" she really is. He says something smooth. She laughs. He types *HER* number in his cell phone. A loud car pulls up to the traffic light.

Oo-chie wally wally, oo-chie bang bang
oo-chie wally wally...
He really really really taught me how to work my body
He really really really taught me how to do it with my mouth
He really really really tried to hurt me hurt me
I really love his thug and gangsta style. [6]

This song, reminiscent of a childhood stepping rhythm, stirs all the girls, including "BJ", to chant and wiggle as if the rap group *Bravehearts*, featuring NAS, was playing their anthem.

As I waited at the bus stop, fifty questions popped into my mind. *Wow, I thought, was that me? Was I like that? Where is "BJ's" mom? What would she think about this? Did she want him to "hurt HER... hurt HER?" How about HER dad? Did HER dad tell HER that guys had the authority to touch HER like that? Or did HER dad touch HER in the same inappropriate way? Or did HER father lack the emotional capacity to tell HER the truth, as did mine? Where did she learn that behavior? Where did he learn that he had the right to act as he did? Why did he feel that he could call HER "Phat ass" and that she would respond positively? Why did she stop? Did he see HER face, or did it even matter? Did he care how old she was? Would they "fuck"?*
Would he wear a condom? Does he have kids? Does she have HIV?

Celebrate HER Now!

I wanted to sit *HER* down and ask, "Hey lil' sis, what's your name? Did he ask your name? Did he even look at your face? This is your body, you know, and people should only touch it when you want them to. Would you have stopped to talk to him if he called you, 'beautiful'?"

But I said nothing; I just let *HER* walk away with *HER* friends. After that encounter, I realized that I needed to find a way to create a space to help *HER* and those like *HER* to understand and acknowledge their beauty and value: *Sisters' Sanctuary*^{TM}!

*

When one thinks of making copies, one thinks of *Xerox*. When one thinks of Bleach, one thinks of *Clorox*. Bandages, *Band-Aid*. Certain kinds of suggestive music have become so powerful that Black women are now synonymous with hoes, whores, and bitches.

Where is *HER* sacredness? Not in music, rarely on film, and most likely, not in *HER* community. Do Black mothers call their daughters beautiful? Do mothers *believe* they are beautiful? Who protected Mom from this degradation in *HER* generation?

We have allowed media to define the Black woman and our girls, and young men have crafted their very identity on the fantasies they see on television and hear on the radio. Who guides them otherwise?

Hip-Hop is ubiquitous. The generation of people born between 1980 and 1993 is influenced to purchase everything from soft drinks to clothing via Hip-Hop. It has become a culture, a mind-set where women are objects and adornments for men's egos and fantasies.

Hip-Hop has become a religion. Commercial Hip-Hop has become a worldwide phenomenon that defines Black women and men as animalistic and carnal.

*

Jill Scott's poem, *The Thickness,* was not just speaking of me when it said *"She a big chick, big o' legs, big o' thighs, big o' hips, big o' ass, big o' tits, She so big! Won't nobody even try to reach HER mind."* She is speaking about the millions of "BJ's" that feel special and beautiful when men of all ages acknowledge them, no matter how offensive and derogatory the comments or actions. She is speaking about the girls who are starving for attention, to be noticed, and don't know any other way but to flash a thong, "drop down and get *HER* eagle on"[8] or act out the lyrics to songs that beat *HER* spirit down all day long.

Sisters' Sanctuary[TM] shows *HER* that she has a **CHOICE.**

Sisters' Sanctuary[TM] *...because I am sacred.*[TM]

Our Sacredness is urgent.

MISSION 1

I LOVE MYSELF BECAUSE...

Lacey C. Clark!

I DESERVE
AND WILL CREATE
A SPECIAL SPACE FOR ME!

Notes:

_____
_____
_____
_____
_____
_____
_____
_____
_____
_____
_____
_____
_____
_____
_____
_____
_____
_____
_____
_____
_____
_____
_____
_____
_____
_____

Create your own sanctuary, a sacred space where you can retreat. Engage four of your five senses: touch, sight, smell and sound. Serene music and pleasant imagery may be used.

Your space should incorporate the four elements of nature (earth, wind, fire and water).

- **Earth** - Incense, sand, plants or soil (smell and sight)
- **Fire** - Candle (sight)
- **Water** - Waterfall, bowl of Sea Salt and water for cleaning negative energy (sound and touch)
- **Wind** - Good circulation and/or wind chimes (sound and touch)

Create a soothing space that speaks to your most beautiful self. It should be quiet, clean and just for you. It may include affirmations and pictures of people who inspire you. Cover your sacred space with a plush rug or carpet (touch). If you are really creative you may install a faux beach theme with real sand as your floor.

Your creative possibilities are endless. Be sure to keep it simple enough to create and maintain. It is not about spending a lot of money, but about beautifying a space that is just for you.

Those in your home should respect that this is your sacred space that should not be used for anything else. This will be a place to sit in stillness, uninterrupted by cell phones and excess noise, a place to turn off all contact with the world and listen to you. Things that make you feel beautiful and remind you of peace and goodness should surround your sanctuary.

Lacey C. Clark!

Chakras are energy centers or energy wheels that spin and exist within our body. They are part of our non-material self. The seven energy centers correspond to ways of being and body parts. Each chakra corresponds to the colors of the rainbow and ascends through our body in the order given by the ROYGBIV acronym: Red, Orange, Yellow, Green, Blue, Indigo, and Violet.

These colors correlate to musical frequencies, or notes. Using these colors can aid you in creating a harmonious environment and in focusing on your personal areas of improvement.

Basic Color Meanings and Their Chakras

RED - the color of the root chakra and the musical note "C". The ROOT chakra, also called the FIRST or BASE chakra, is located at the base of the spine. It is associated with issues of survival, passion, drive, and ambition, grounding one's energy in the physical dimension; one's life forces, and balancing experiences that create "fight or flight."

ORANGE - the color of the sacral or second chakra and the musical note "D". The SACRAL chakra, also called the SECOND chakra or the SEXUAL chakra, is positioned in the area between the navel and the pubic bone. Depending on which sources you read, it can be shown to be centered on the navel itself or to be aligned with the sexual organs, ovaries in women and testes in men. It is associated with creativity, sexuality, relationships, and reproduction.

YELLOW - the color of the solar plexus chakra and the musical note "E". The SOLAR PLEXUS chakra or THIRD chakra is located midway between the end of the breastbone and the navel. It is associated with issues of personal power, emotions (especially blocked emotions), passion for living, and the ability to protect oneself from being the target of negative or aggressive emotions.

30

GREEN - the color of the heart chakra and the musical note "F". Sometimes the heart chakra is shown as pink, especially in relation to sending love out from the heart. The HEART chakra is positioned in the center of the chest, usually shown to be even with the nipple line. The heart is associated with compassion, friendship, empathy and the ability to give and receive love.

AZURE BLUE - the color of the throat chakra and the musical note "G". The THROAT chakra is positioned at the base of throat. It is associated with communication, expression and speaking one's truth.

INDIGO BLUE - the color of the third eye chakra and the musical note "A". The THIRD EYE chakra is located in the center of the forehead. This chakra is also called the AJNA center. It is associated with intuition, understanding, visualization, and inner vision.

VIOLET - the color of the crown chakra and the musical note "B". The CROWN chakra or HEAD chakra is positioned at the top of the head. It is associated with cosmic awareness, highest spirituality, and complete integration with Source.

If you have been feeling sluggish and need to feel energized and charged try adding a power color like red or orange to your atmosphere.

If you are stressed and having problems communicating, try incorporating blue into your atmosphere.

How can you incorporate the colors into your healing experiences?

_____
_____
_____
_____
_____
_____
_____
_____
_____
_____
_____
_____
_____

How will you use them in your sanctuary?

_____
_____
_____
_____
_____
_____
_____
_____
_____
_____
_____
_____
_____
_____
_____
_____

Design your sacred space here. Use magazine cutouts to bring your sacred space to a reality on paper first. Replicate this image in your real space one step at a time. Remember to keep it simple.

Checklist For Sacred Space

- ☐ Identify where your sacred space will be. (Choose a space with good light and away from noise.)
- ☐ Clean and clear your space from anything that does not speak to your mission of peace and solitude.
- ☐ Gather pictures and empowering words that you want to see in your sacred space.
- ☐ Identify your colors.
- ☐ Collect the items you want to include, i.e. plants, fabric, candles, seashells, etc.
- ☐ Begin installation. Play your favorite soft music or build your space in silence.
- ☐ Enjoy your space. Sit down. Sit still and be with you.

Self-Work:

Meditation #1- Breathe deeply and slowly in through your nose as if smelling a room full of roses. Hold for 4 counts. Exhale slowly, breathing out all of the stress and anxiety from the day. Repeat 20 times and increase the number of breaths every week.

Meditation #2- Flame staring. Sit in a comfortable position with your back straight. Breathe deeply and stare at the white part of the flame just above the wick. Stay focused on that area for 5-10 minutes but try your best to forget about time and just be one with your flame. Continue to stare and breathe deeply.

In your sanctuary, practice active listening skills. Try a *Talk Fast* also known as a Vow of Silence. Why? Because sometimes we talk too much and listen too little. Sometimes we talk so much that we don't even realize it. We must get a grip on our mouths. Let us be quiet for about two days straight. That's right, ladies!

Celebrate HER Now!

Absolutely no talking for 48 hours! Take a vow of silence and promise yourself that you will be meditative, introspective, and pensive for the right direction of your life. Forewarn your friends and families via email and phone calls the night before. If you have other members in your household, write notes and letters explaining directions. Most importantly listen, observe, and pay attention to you and the world inside and out. If you work a 9-5, it may be best to schedule this activity on the weekend. If you have errands to run, you may want to wear a small alert pin (www.sisterssanctuary.org), indicating that you are not speaking for two days.

Day One - If you accidentally speak forgive yourself and quickly go back to where you were.

What are you experiencing? What are you discovering? Write your thoughts and experiences here:

_____

_____

_____

_____

_____

_____

_____

_____

_____

_____

_____

_____

_____

_____

_____

_____

Day Two

_____
_____
_____
_____
_____
_____
_____
_____
_____
_____
_____
_____
_____
_____
_____
_____

When your fast is over, cut the gossip and stop perpetuating stereotypes. "Women are catty" or "Bitches always hatin'." We have the power to break that stereotype by not running our mouths about anyone else but ourselves. When we do speak, it should be about how we are growing not about what is going wrong. Focus on speaking purposefully and intently.

Try not to waste words or energy on the lives of "Tammy, Tanel and Tiffany." They have their own bridges to cross and struggles to overcome. No one is perfect, not even you. Speak beauty and positivity in the universe… and it will speak back!

What have you done with the time you saved gossiping?

_____
_____
_____
_____
_____

Celebrate HER Now!

How does if feel to step closer to you via your physical sanctuary? What have you created by saving your verbal energy?

_____

_____

_____

_____

_____

_____

_____

_____

_____

_____

_____

_____

_____

_____

_____

_____

_____

_____

_____

_____

_____

_____

_____

_____

_____

_____

_____

_____

_____

_____

_____

_____

_____

Lacey C. Clark!

I AM MY OWN CELEBRITY!

Notes:

_____
_____
_____
_____
_____
_____
_____
_____
_____
_____
_____
_____
_____
_____
_____
_____
_____
_____
_____
_____
_____
_____
_____
_____
_____
_____

Develop low-cost pampering ritual activities that make you feel like your very own Halle Berry, Beyonce', and Oprah. Often times we envy celebrities because they seem to have it all. They are the pampered and celebrated people.

But, what can you do to make *you* feel good? How can you cater to your needs? Celebrate yourself? Perhaps it's a foot or hand massage, taking an aromatherapy bath, or writing a personal love letter to you. Whatever it is, fully immerse yourself in the moment of your personal pleasure.

Aromatherapy literally means healing through scents. Aromatherapy was used by the most ancient civilizations: Egypt, China, and India, and is reputed to be at least 6,000 years old. Our foremothers and fathers used the essences of flowers and other plants to cleanse, bring good energy, revive, celebrate, mourn, and heal. They used scents for just about anything.

Aromatherapy began with the Ancient Egyptians who extracted oils from aromatic plants that were used for medicinal and cosmetic purposes as well as embalming. Ancient Egyptians used scents of specific plants for religious rituals because certain smells could raise higher consciousness or promote a state of tranquility.

Frankincense was burned at dawn as an offering to the sun and myrrh was offered to the moon. The Egyptians were experts at embalming and used oils and scents in the mummification process. They used herbs like peppermint and ginger to aid digestive processes, protect against infection, and build the immune system. After bathing, the Egyptians used fragrant oils to massage themselves.

Here are some oils and their basic uses:

RELAXING:

- ❖ Lavender (also antiseptic)
- ❖ Chamomile
- ❖ Jasmine
- ❖ Frankincense and myrrh (both can irritate when used on the skin or in the bath)
- ❖ Neroli
- ❖ Orange or tangerine
- ❖ Ylang-ylang (over-inhalation may cause headaches)

STIMULATING:

- ❖ Peppermint and eucalyptus (both act as decongestant when inhaled, but may irritate the skin, so be cautious)

REVITALIZING:

- ❖ Lemon (may irritate the skin, especially when exposed to the sun)
- ❖ Grapefruit
- ❖ Cinnamon
- ❖ Juniper (also has antiseptic properties)
- ❖ Vanilla
- ❖ Geranium
- ❖ Rosemary

Other oils such as tea-tree oil are renowned for their antiseptic properties. All essential oils are highly concentrated, so please use them as directed. The bottles should indicate specific warnings but as an extra precaution keep all oils away from pregnant women and children.

Here are basic recipes for you to enjoy and incorporate into your pampering ritual.

Aromatherapy Body Powder (Good for your feet!)

- 1 cup Cornstarch
- 1 tablespoon Baking Soda
- 1 jar with a tight fitting lid
- Add 15-20 drops of your favorite essential oils

Mix ingredients together and shake well.

Basic Bath Salts

- 1 cup Sea Salt
- 1 cup Epsom Salt
- 1 cup Baking Soda
- Your favorite essential oils (Try Rose, Geranium, Lavender, and/or Ylang-Ylang.)
- 6 drops of essential oils per 1/4 cup salt blend

This makes enough for several baths. Use 1/4 cup per bath.

Soothing Lavender Honey Bath

Did you know that honey has a calming effect? Combined with pure essential oil of lavender it's an awesome bath treatment. Why not try it tonight?

- 2 oz. of Honey
- 5 drops Lavender

Combine in a jar. Use 1 -2 Tablespoons per bath. Please do not drink!

Self-Love Body Massage Oil Blend *(Non-Sexual)*

- 4 drops of Rose oil
- 6 drops of Sandalwood
- 1 drop of Ylang Ylang
- About six teaspoons of carrier oil

Percentage should equal about 2 to 3 drops of essential oil per teaspoon of vegetable oil (known as carrier oil) base such as Sweet Almond Oil, Avocado Oil or Grapeseed Oil (about six teaspoons).

How did you feel after your Lavender Honey bath treat?

_____
_____
_____
_____
_____
_____
_____
_____

What were you thinking about while soaking in the Lavender Honey bath treatment?

_____
_____
_____
_____
_____
_____
_____
_____
_____
_____
_____

_____

_____

How about your self-love massage?

_____

_____

_____

_____

_____

_____

_____

_____

_____

_____

_____

_____

_____

_____

_____

How did it feel to touch yourself in a non-sexual way?

_____

_____

_____

_____

_____

_____

_____

_____

_____

_____

_____

_____

Lacey C. Clark!

I AM WORTHY OF WHOLESOME FOODS THAT COMPLEMENT MY GREATNESS...

I EAT TO LIVE NOT LIVE TO EAT!

Notes:

_____
_____
_____
_____
_____
_____
_____
_____
_____
_____
_____
_____
_____
_____
_____
_____
_____
_____
_____
_____
_____
_____
_____
_____

Eat Right

You can't be on the right path when your daily diet consists of pizza and cigarettes! According to the National Center of Health Statistics, heart disease is the leading cause of death for African-American women. The U.S. Department of Health and Human Services states that the incidence of diabetes in African-American women is 85% higher than that in Caucasian women. In fact, mortality rates for African-American women are higher than those for any other racial/ethnic group for nearly every major cause of death including heart disease, lung cancer, cerebrovascular disease, breast cancer, and chronic obstructive pulmonary diseases.

To combat these dis-eases, build up your strength and your resistance to these life-threatening illnesses! Eat plenty of fruit, lightly steamed veggies, legumes, baked fish, and poultry. Drink lots of water (at least half your body weight in ounces each day), and avoid cakes, breads, and sweets. Get plenty of exercise and adequate sleep... Love your heart and your health, and they will love you back!

What are you eating? Dr. Laila Afrika, in his book, <u>African Holistic Health</u>, highlights some important dietary guidelines for people of African descent:

"Blacks have specific nutritional and dietary needs. These nutritional needs arise because we have specific bodily differences as compared to other races and cultures. For example, over 70% of Black people (worldwide) cannot digest cattle milk. In addition, the intestinal florae (bacteria, virus, fungus and yeast) that naturally live in Black people's intestines are unique to Blacks. Subsequently, Blacks assimilate food in the intestines differently. Also, despite centuries of living in countries outside of Africa, their intestinal florae are the same as it was in their ancestor's stomachs 2,000 years ago in Africa.

"Melanin (black color pigment) is obviously most abundant in Blacks. This melanin aids in protecting Blacks from the ultraviolet rays of the sun. It also increases the speed of nerve and brain messages, which are transmitted between the left and right hemispheres of the brain and all nerve signals transmitted throughout the bodily nerve network... Black people's blood crystallizes differently from Caucasian's blood. These are some of the many reasons why Blacks have unique nutritional, medical, and dietary needs." [9]

For more information on the above statistics, see *Making the Grade on Women's Health: A National and State-by-State Report Card:* (Washington: National Women's Law Center, August 2000) [10]

Do you think it is possible that hypertension, heart disease, cancer, diabetes, rheumatic diseases, gastrointestinal disorders, and skin disorders are related directly or indirectly to our diets?

Most of what we know as soul food is actually slave food - scraps left over from what the slave master didn't want. Traditional 'soul food' includes hog maws, ham, pork chops, chitterlings, pig feet, and cornbread. It is usually prepared with pork fat, lard, milk, eggs, butter, salt, and lots of refined (white) sugar. These ingredients are not compatible with our biochemical makeup, and diets that rely too heavily on them may lead to some of the many diseases that we suffer from today.

Celebrate HER Now!

What small but progressive changes can you make towards your diet?

Please circle the healthiest choice:

1. Orange Soda   *Kool-Aid*   Orange Juice   Water

2. Fried Chicken   Fried Shrimp   Fried Pork Chop   Baked Fish

3. French Fries   Baked Potato   Mashed Potatoes w/ butter and salt

4. Twinkies   Fruit Parfait   Cupcakes   Ice cream

5. Collard Greens with Fat Back   Steamed Broccoli   Candied carrots

Here are a few healthy recipes that you can prepare as alternatives to some of those harmful foods mentioned above.

Cheeseburger Alternative: Prepare broiled or grilled chicken or fish sandwiches. Serve with mustard instead of mayonnaise.

French Fries Alternative: Baked Sweet Potato "Fries"

- Boil sweet potatoes until soft, and then cool completely in refrigerator.

- Slice into wedges.

- Grill in nonstick pan on medium to high heat until browned.

- Season with salt and pepper as desired.

-Courtesy of Kindcafe.com

Soda Alternative: Dilute unsweetened fruit juice with water or seltzer to decrease sugar intake. Drink water with a squeeze of lemon, or try herbal teas (hot or cold). Drinking fresh vegetable juice is also a good low-sugar alternative to soda or juice. Sweeten teas with Stevia, an herb that is 100 times sweeter than sugar but without any calories. Available in liquid or powdered form, it comes in packets and can be found at health food stores and even some grocery stores. But, it is an acquired taste.

Fried Chicken Alternative: "Oven Fried Chicken"

- broiler-fryer chicken, about 2 to 2 1/2 cups, cut into 8 pieces

- 1/2 cup fine dry bread crumbs

- 2 teaspoons salt

- teaspoon paprika

- 1/4 teaspoon pepper

- 1/4 cup vegetable oil

PREPARATION:

Wash chicken pieces; pat dry. Combine breadcrumbs, salt, paprika and pepper. Brush each piece of chicken with vegetable oil, and then roll in crumb mixture. Place in shallow baking pan, skin side up. Bake at 425° for about 30 to 35 minutes, or until chicken is tender and juices run clear.

Collard Greens with Fat Back Alternative: Mean Smoked Greens

- 1 tablespoon olive oil
- 1 cup chopped onion

- 2 cloves garlic
- 2 pounds collard greens - rinsed, trimmed and chopped
- 1 tablespoon brown sugar
- 1 tablespoon molasses
- 1 tablespoon liquid smoke flavoring
- Salt and ground black pepper to taste

Heat oil in a large pot. Sauté onion and garlic until onions are translucent. Place chopped collard greens in pot, and add enough water to cover the greens. Stir in brown sugar, molasses and liquid smoke. Season with salt and pepper. Bring to a boil, reduce heat, and simmer for 30 to 40 minutes, or until greens are tender.

NOTE: Burning hickory chips, then condensing the smoke into a liquid form, produces liquid smoke. The liquid is then filtered to remove all impurities. You can find it in most grocery stores in the section with the barbeque sauce and steak sauce. Some brands are more concentrated than others, so use wisely.

Sweets Alternative: Sweet Potato Pie
- 1 cup cooked, mashed sweet potatoes
- 1 tbsp soy margarine, softened
- ½ cup silken tofu, drained
- 1 cup vanilla soy milk
- ½ cup maple syrup (or more, to taste)
- 1 tsp vanilla extract
- 1 tsp cinnamon
- ½ tsp sea salt
- ¼ tsp ground ginger
- ¼ tsp nutmeg
- 1 unbaked 9-inch whole wheat pie crust

Sweet Cream Topping

- ½ pound firm tofu
- ¼ cup vegetable oil
- ¼ cup maple syrup (to taste)
- 1tsp vanilla extract
- ½ tsp lemon juice
- 1/8 tsp salt

Preheat oven to 350 degrees. In a large mixing bowl, combine sweet potatoes and soy margarine in a blender or food processor. Blend in tofu. Add soymilk, maple syrup, vanilla, cinnamon, salt, ginger and nutmeg, mixing until well blended. Pour the filling into the crust and bake for 45 to 50 minutes or until firm. For Sweet Cream Topping, blend all ingredients until smooth and creamy. Chill prepared topping before serving with pie. Pie serves 4; topping recipe yields 1½ cups.

- Adapted from 366 Simply Delicious Dairy-Free Recipes by Robin Robertson [11]

- From Blackvegatrians.org

I know you may be thinking that making better choices about food is something that does not interest you, but think about those statistics. We have the power to change our relationship to food and our eating habits for ourselves and for the next generation. I encourage you to have fun when preparing these recipes and be open-minded because these recipes maybe different from your normal eating habits. For more healthy recipes, visit us at www.sisterssanctuary.org.

I AM LEGENDARY…

I ENJOY BEING
WITH ME!

Lacey C. Clark!

Notes:

_____
_____
_____
_____
_____
_____
_____
_____
_____
_____
_____
_____
_____
_____
_____
_____
_____
_____
_____
_____
_____
_____
_____
_____
_____

On your ideal date what would your partner do for you that would make you feel special, beautiful, and loved in a non-sexual way? Close you eyes and visualize this experience right now. What is your partner wearing, what is s/he doing? What are you wearing? Where are you? What are you doing?

Open your eyes and think about how to do the same thing for yourself.

_____
_____
_____
_____
_____
_____
_____
_____
_____
_____
_____
_____
_____

Self–Date = enjoying your own company

We often define ourselves based on our circle of friends. We become attached to others via their way of thinking, their style of dress, and their social activities. What do **you** like to do?
- ≠ Do you have to hang out with Denise, Tanya and Cheryl all the time?
- ≠ Do you even like (un) Happy Hour?
- ≠ Can you enjoy your own company?
- ≠ Can you feel happy and fulfilled without a mate?

Lacey C. Clark!

As our youth would say... **Do You!** Take yourself out on a date. We go all out for the family vacation, plan everyone else's time... you deserve to plan your time. Put the same energy that you would put into that family trip into your date. The preparation should be just as important as the actual event. Book reservations, schedule a spa appointment, and send yourself an itinerary on fine stationery. If you will be spending time at home, clean up like you would if you had company. Set the table... sip some of your favorite wine or beverage. Go to a concert and dance in the aisles, go skating and eat popcorn. People watch. Listen to your favorite song while preparing your favorite foot soak. Have a blast with you. Don't forget to buy yourself flowers.

As women we often wait in the wings for something magical to happen! We are magic. Define your pleasure. The best way to accomplish this is by experimenting. We won't know what we like until we try it!

At this time please pull out your planner. What are you doing with your time?

_____
_____
_____
_____
_____
_____
_____
_____
_____
_____
_____

Can you schedule time to get away from the hustle and bustle of life? (i.e. for an hour a day, or perhaps for 2 hours on a weekend)?

When is your next or first self-date? Please write date and time down now.

_____ / _____ / _____

What can you do to enjoy yourself?

Chart your first self-date itinerary here:

What	When	Where	Why	Investment$

Self-Dating Checklist

- ❏ Make a date

- ❏ Make reservations.

- ❏ Clear out your schedule for that time or on that day.

- ❏ Order some flowers to be sent to wherever you are.

- ❏ Pick out your favorite outfit and underwear. Make sure they are comfortable.

- ❏ Pull out your favorite scents and lotions and make this part of the experience.

- ❏ As a safety precaution, be sure to tell a close friend or family member where you plan to go and what time you plan to return.

- ❏ Cut your mobile contact devices off for true peace of mind.

EX: Go out on a date and paste your memorabilia (i.e., ticket

stubs, receipts, picture etc.) here.

How did you feel on your self-date? What did you do? Who did you meet (non-romantic)?

_____

_____

_____

_____

_____

_____

_____

Were you embarrassed to eat in a restaurant or sit in a movie by yourself? Why or why not?

_____

_____

_____

_____

_____

_____

_____

_____

_____

_____

How did you feel when you saw couples interacting?

_____

_____

_____

_____

_____

_____

_____

_____

_____

Lacey C. Clark!

I HIGHLIGHT MY PAST AND PRESENT ACCOMPLISHMENTS BUT I AM STILL OPEN FOR GROWTH!

Notes:

_____

_____

_____

_____

_____

_____

_____

_____

_____

_____

_____

_____

_____

_____

_____

_____

_____

_____

_____

_____

_____

_____

_____

_____

_____

_____

Celebrate HER Now!

Create a personal inventory of your strengths and areas for growth. In what areas in life do you shine? Everyone shines at something... if you don't know where you shine, then do an investigation: ask your relatives and your closest friends how you have shone in your past.

Once you define your strengths be sure to define areas in need of improvement. Don't be afraid to delegate responsibility to someone who can support your areas of development.

Look through your old childhood awards and certificates and revisit what you were praised for in the past. Did you win a basketball tournament? Did you have perfect attendance? Where you good at track? What about your grades? Many of these skills are probably still with you. Dust off the layers of life's obstacles and uncover your individual greatness.

Here are some triggers that will help you in this process:

- What books did you read?
- What T.V. shows did you watch?
- What games did you play?
- What were your favorite songs?
- Your favorite movie?
- Favorite Food?
- Favorite Pet?
- Favorite Color?

List your accomplishments for the following time periods:

Years: 19_____ to 19_____
0-10 years

_____
_____
_____
_____

Lacey C. Clark!

Years: 19 _____ to _____
11-20 years

_____
_____
_____
_____
_____

Years: _____ to _____
21-30 years

_____
_____
_____
_____
_____

Years: _____ to _____
31-40 years

_____
_____
_____
_____
_____

Years: _____ to _____
41-50 years

_____
_____
_____
_____
_____

Years: _____ to _____
51-60 years

_____
_____
_____
_____
_____
_____
_____
_____

Years: _____ to _____
60-70 years

_____
_____
_____
_____
_____
_____
_____
_____

Years: _____ to _____
71- to present

_____
_____
_____
_____
_____
_____
_____
_____

What skills have you discovered or rediscovered as a result of your thinking about your past accomplishments? How did the triggers make you feel?

_____

_____

_____

_____

_____

How can you apply these accomplishments and skills to your career, child- rearing, love life, and spiritual development?

_____

_____

_____

_____

_____

_____

_____

_____

_____

* Memory Net process Adapted from "What Color Is Your Parachute?" [12] by Richard N. Bolles

MY CLOTHING REFLECTS THE BEAUTIFUL LAYERS OF MY HUMANITY…

NOT JUST MY SEXUALITY!

Notes:

_____
_____
_____
_____
_____
_____
_____
_____
_____
_____
_____
_____
_____
_____
_____
_____
_____
_____
_____
_____
_____
_____
_____
_____
_____

Clothing SPEAKS VOLUMES. What you are wearing might determine whether or not someone takes you seriously or respects you for the dynamic human being that you are. What we wear can communicate these distinct messages:

Tight pants of any kind, especially if you are hippy or if you wear pants with any kind of writing on the butt, no matter how intellectual or school spirited, is clearly advertising your butt.

T-shirts that say something like "My heart belongs to what's his name", "I'm Hot, You're Not", "I'll try anything once", "I don't know what I'm doing", "Bootilicious", "I'm Flexible", "Lick Me!" or "Property of Playboy" suggest promiscuity and attract sexual attention. These messages contribute to the objectification of women and girls. They contribute to the perception of women as walking sex objects. When we as women, wear these kinds of clothes, we rear our children to walk in that same carnal, superficial, and sexual legacy.

What subtle or obvious messages do you see everyday? What messages have you overlooked?

_____
_____
_____
_____

What kind of attention do you want? Does it match what you are getting?

_____
_____
_____
_____
_____

Lacey C. Clark!

If you want sexual attention, why?

_____
_____
_____
_____
_____
_____
_____
_____

How does it make you feel? Do you think it is okay?

_____
_____
_____
_____
_____
_____
_____

How do you feel in a two-piece executive suit? Swimsuit? Jogging outfit? T-shirt and jeans? Short skirt?

_____
_____
_____
_____
_____
_____
_____
_____
_____

What are you wearing right now? What does it advertise to the world?

_____
_____
_____
_____
_____
_____
_____
_____

What can you wear to get the kind of attention you want?

_____
_____
_____
_____
_____
_____
_____
_____

Self-Work Experiment:

Change your outfits. Experiment with different styles and note the different forms of attention you receive from others.

Lacey C. Clark!

I APPRECIATE THE BEAUTY AND DIVINITY OF MY NATURAL HAIR.

Notes:

_____

_____

_____

_____

_____

_____

_____

_____

_____

_____

_____

_____

_____

_____

_____

_____

_____

_____

_____

_____

_____

_____

_____

_____

Good Hair is hair that is growing healthy and strong in its natural state. Did you know that the hair we call nappy is the hair structure that resembles the DNA pattern, and the spiral pattern for cosmic energy?

When the wind moves, it moves in a spiral form. Our hair replicates that spiral movement and we hate it! The spiral is the simplest and most common geometric shape in nature, visible or invisible. From conch shells, to weather patterns, to DNA, to galaxies, spirals are omnipresent in nature. From the movement and awesome power of tornadoes, trees in the mountains growing in a spiral twist to make them stronger when they bend in the wind, and plants spiraling up from the soil, this is nature's organic pattern.

During the Middle Passage (15th-19th Century), we didn't have grooming items to maintain anything, let alone our coifs. During the slave era some of our roles as slaves were to comb the master's wife's hair, and their children's hair. We would comb their hair with a fine-toothcomb (the ones we use today), and then try to run the same comb through our hair to no avail.

Our hair was of course a lot thicker and had a difficult time passing through. Subconsciously and consciously we longed to have the "simplicity" in grooming our hair, so instead of changing the comb we decided to change the texture of our hair via straightening combs and perms. We wanted "massa" to respect us and value us as human beings, so we tried, as we still try today, to be more like him.

"You got good hair." We say this to people with hair farthest from tightly coiled hair. If you choose to "fry, dye and weave to the side," please know that we were taught to think of kinky hair as inferior, horrible and ugly. If you are afraid of your divinity or your GOD–given functional hair, our youths will be afraid as well. Believing that your natural hair is hard to maintain is a myth.

Incorporating wide-toothcombs and hair oil, hair butter, hair milk or good old fashion hair grease into your maintenance routine can easily change that concept. For current maintenance techniques and support for natural hair you can subscribe to *Naturally You Magazine™*. It's 100% you.

What are your hair stories? Do you have a hair "Horror Story"?

_____

_____

_____

_____

_____

_____

_____

_____

When was the first time you got your hair straightened? How about your first perm? Did you let your "Soul Glo" with a Jherri Curl?

_____

_____

_____

_____

_____

_____

_____

_____

What was said about straight hair and those who had it? Write your memories here.

_____

_____

_____

_____

_____

_____

_____

_____

Would you go natural? Why or why not?

_____

_____

_____

_____

_____

_____

_____

In grade school there would usually be at least one girl who wore her hair natural, how did you treat her? How did others treat her?

_____

_____

_____

_____

_____

_____

_____

_____

_____

_____

_____

_____

MY COMPLEXION IS PERFECT FOR ME AND I WILL CELEBRATE IT BECAUSE IT IS A GIFT FROM THE DIVINE.

Notes:

_____

_____

_____

_____

_____

_____

_____

_____

_____

_____

_____

_____

_____

_____

_____

_____

_____

_____

_____

_____

_____

_____

Melanin is powerful! It is the reason why we as people of color age so gracefully without having to use all of the chemical products promising to reduce wrinkles, etc. It is the absorber of the sun. And again we have been taught to measure our standard of beauty against a European aesthetic.

Over the centuries, we have bought billions of dollars worth of creams and potions that bleach our skin. Again, our value judgment was based on a European aesthetic; lighter skin and straighter hair, represented beauty, value, and respect. This value judgment goes beyond this country. In fact, colonization made us hate ourselves worldwide. Our self-hatred even exists on the African continent. To this day, sisters and brothers are using soaps and creams to make their skin lighter. Some have skin so light that it appears orange. The products used are so harsh that it impairs the body's natural ability to heal itself, so if one were to get a cut it would take very long to heal, if at all.

We are beautiful people! But some of us fail to see this! Your skin is amazing; it is in love with the sun. Comments like, "You are pretty, for a dark-skinned person," communicate that dark-skinned people do not have the right to be pretty.

What have you been taught about your skin?
_____
_____
_____
_____
_____
_____
_____
_____
_____

Did your elders place a value judgment on other people based on the color of their skin? If so, ask them why.

_____
_____
_____
_____
_____
_____
_____
_____

What was said about lighter-skinned people?

_____
_____
_____
_____
_____
_____
_____

What was said about darker-skinned people?

_____
_____
_____
_____
_____
_____
_____
_____
_____
_____

Celebrate HER Now!

What kind of beauty products did the women in your family use? Why did they say they were using them?

_____
_____
_____
_____
_____
_____
_____
_____
_____
_____
_____

What was said about your complexion?

_____
_____
_____
_____
_____
_____
_____
_____
_____
_____
_____

Turn negative comments into affirmations.

Insult: Tar Baby
Affirmation: SAY IT LOUD, I'M BLACK AND I'M PROUD!

Insult: Casper
Affirmation: My skin color is perfect for my mission in this lifetime and I am proud of it. I am beautiful.

Insult #1:

_____

_____

_____

Affirmation:

_____

_____

_____

Insult #2:

_____

_____

_____

Affirmation:

_____

_____

_____

Insult #3:

_____

_____

_____

Affirmation:

_____

_____

_____

Insult #4:

_____
_____
_____

Affirmation:

_____
_____
_____

Insult #5:

_____
_____
_____

Affirmation:

_____
_____
_____

Make a list of all of your partners/mates. Chart their complexions.

Name	Complexion

Make a list of all of your friends. Chart their complexions as well.

Name	Complexion

Do you see any patterns? What are they? If so, why?

_____

_____

_____

_____

THIS IS MY BODY: A BEAUTIFUL PLACE FOR HEALING, BIRTH, AND CLEANSING...

A PLACE OF HONOR!

Notes:

_____
_____
_____
_____
_____
_____
_____
_____
_____
_____
_____
_____
_____
_____
_____
_____
_____
_____
_____
_____
_____
_____
_____
_____
_____
_____

Does your body belong to you? Do you know it? For so long, our bodies have not been ours. During the institution of slavery, one of the ways to show that we were property, was to treat our bodies as such. Our bodies were used to toil the fields from sun up to sun down, as wet nurses for the masters' white children, as whipping posts for brutal blood-drawing beatings, and as "fuck holes" to rape and deposit unwanted semen.

For centuries we have carried this shame, this pain, this neglect. This pain comes in the form of silence, when someone touches us inappropriately. It shows up when our mothers don't have the courage to talk about periods or the time when her uncle Jay molested her. It comes in the form of not being able to look at your naked body in the mirror and celebrate it, appreciate it, and honor it. It even shows up when we consistently put our bodies' sexuality on display with tight fitted clothing.

Explore your body. Touch yourself... How do you feel? What do you smell like? How does your vagina look? Your elbows, Your back? Your body is a work of art, and all beautiful art pieces need attention, care, and someone to respect them... that someone is you. Own your body! It is yours.

The first time I realized that my body was as beautiful as anyone else's in spite of the stretch marks and discolorations was when I visited a women's day event at a bathhouse in New York City. I was told that a bathing suit was optional. My good friend Nikki and I knew we were going to keep our bathing suits on... especially because we're both plus sized women.

We arrived at the bathhouse and went to the locker room and began to get situated with our bathing suits when I said, "You know what Nikki? I'm going nude."

She giggled. "Oh my GOD, chile', I can't believe... chile'... okay... let's do it." We giggled all the way to the bathhouse quarters.

We met so many amazing women, and they too, were nude and Black. They were walking and talking in the saunas like they had clothes on. I was so shocked, but also felt honored and free. This feeling was awesome, liberating... everybody's body was different. Short, tall, fat, skinny, white, black, hairy, bald, one breast, two breasts, straight backed, curved back, old and young.

Wow, there was no sexual association, no reason to suck my stomach in, or lift my breasts up... my body was able to breathe and live amongst other bodies. It was one of the most beautiful experiences of my life. It helped me see that **everyBODY** has a BODY and that this is the shell that we are given in this lifetime. What a wonderful shell it is.

My friend Nikki has gone on to celebrate her plus-sized body via nude modeling for visual artists - not pornography... there is a difference. Pornography = any writing or materials meant for sexual arousal, usually defined within patriarchal standard. Nudity = unclothed body. And I have taken advantage of every opportunity to celebrate my body in the nude.

What have you been taught about your body?

_____
_____
_____
_____
_____
_____
_____
_____

Did you use a separate washcloth to wash your vagina? Where did you learn about your private parts and what did you learn? What were they called and by whom?

_____

_____

_____

_____

_____

_____

_____

_____

List your nicknames for your vagina here.
Example: Cutty cat, pocket book, poo-poo, tooch.

1. _____
2. _____
3. _____
4. _____
5. _____

List your nicknames for your breast here.
Example: Boobies, knobs, ninnies, titties, knockers

1. _____
2. _____
3. _____
4. _____
5. _____

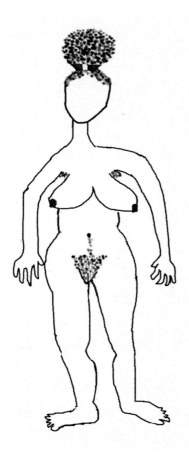

Know your body

If your youth has gumption to ask you about sexuality or sex you should be comfortable enough with your body to talk about your experiences. What makes you tick? What don't you like? Can you share your preferences with ease, or are you inhibited in being honest with what you want? Tell her the truth about where you are, but also tell her where you want to be.

Please use your favorite or most decorative hand mirror and explore your divine, awesome, beautiful human body.

Body Exploration

When I look at my toes I see:

_____

_____

_____

I like my toes because:

_____

_____

_____

When I look at my feet I see:

_____

_____

_____

I like my feet because:

_____

_____

_____

When I look at my calves I see:

_____

_____

_____

I like my calves because:

_____

_____

_____

When I look at my knees I see:

_____

_____

_____

I like my knees because:

_____
_____
_____

When I look at my thighs I see:

_____
_____
_____

I like my thighs because:

_____
_____
_____

When I look at my hips I see:

_____
_____
_____

I like my hips because:

_____
_____
_____

When I look at my vagina I see:

_____
_____
_____

I like my vagina because:

_____
_____
_____

Celebrate HER Now!

When I look at my buttocks I see:

_____
_____
_____

I like my buttocks because:

_____
_____
_____

When I look at my waist I see:

_____
_____
_____

I like my waist because:

_____
_____
_____

When I look at my stomach I see:

_____
_____
_____

I like my stomach because:

_____
_____
_____

When I look at my back I see:

_____
_____
_____

I like my back because:

_____
_____
_____

When I look at my breasts I see:

_____
_____
_____

I like my breasts because:

_____
_____
_____

When I look at my fingers I see:

_____
_____
_____

I like my fingers because:

_____
_____
_____

When I look at my hands I see:

_____
_____
_____

I like my hands because:

_____
_____
_____

Celebrate HER Now!

When I look at my elbows I see:

_____
_____
_____

I like my elbows because:

_____
_____
_____

When I look at my arms I see:

_____
_____
_____

I like my arms because:

_____
_____
_____

When I look at my neck I see:

_____
_____
_____

I like my neck because:

_____
_____
_____

When I look at my ears I see:

_____
_____
_____

I like my ears because:

_____

_____

_____

When I look at my chin I see:

_____

_____

_____

I like my chin because:

_____

_____

_____

When I look at my nose I see:

_____

_____

_____

I like my nose because:

_____

_____

_____

When I look at my eyes I see:

_____

_____

_____

I like my eyes because:

_____

_____

_____

Celebrate HER Now!

When I look at my lips I see:

_____

_____

_____

I like my lips because:

_____

_____

_____

When I look at my eyebrows I see:

_____

_____

_____

I like my eyebrows because:

_____

_____

_____

When I look at my forehead I see:

_____

_____

_____

I like my forehead because:

_____

_____

_____

Find some reason to love your divinely appointed body parts. Remember this is **YOUR** shell. Celebrate IT!

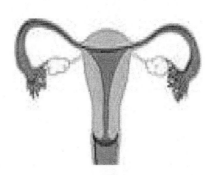

Can you identify the various parts of the womb?

The power of your womb.
It has been shown that calendar consciousness developed first in women because of their natural body rhythms, which corresponded to the phases of the moon.

What are/were your thoughts about your period?

_____
_____
_____
_____
_____
_____
_____
_____

How and where were you introduced to menstruation?

_____
_____
_____

What kind of feelings surrounded this part of your life?

_____
_____
_____

Who first told you about it?

_____

_____

_____

What did they call it?

_____

_____

_____

How does your mate feel about your period?

_____

_____

_____

What impact has media/advertising had on your knowledge and attitude?

_____

_____

_____

Is your experience different now compared to earlier in your life?

_____

_____

_____

Here are some natural options to alleviate menstrual cramps/discomfort:

- Increase exercise. This will improve blood and oxygen circulation throughout the body, including the pelvis.

- Try not to use tampons. Many women find tampons increase cramping.

- Avoid red meat, refined sugars, dairy products, and fatty foods.

- Eat lots of fresh vegetables, whole grains (especially if you experience constipation or indigestion), nuts, seeds, and fruit.

- Avoid caffeine. It constricts blood vessels and increases tension.

- Meditate, or get a massage. Breathe deeply, relax, notice where you hold tension in your body and let it go.

- Drink chamomile tea before, after, and during your period.

- Put cayenne pepper on food. It improves circulation.

SELF-WORK: Write a thank you/apology/love letter/poem/story to your body/womb/vagina explaining your connection or lack thereof. The assignment can be written in the bathtub during your bath treat or in any other warm and sacred space.

DEAR_____

_____
_____
_____
_____
_____
_____
_____
_____
_____
_____
_____

I AM WORTHY OF RE/DEFINING MYSELF FOR MYSELF.

Notes:

_____
_____
_____
_____
_____
_____
_____
_____
_____
_____
_____
_____
_____
_____
_____
_____
_____
_____
_____
_____
_____
_____
_____
_____

As I waited patiently at the bus stop, two guys in their late twenties, high on weed or some other downer, reclining comfortably in their car seats, pulled up and asked if I knew the directions to a specific nightclub. I didn't know where it was exactly, but I politely gave them the general area. The driver responded with, "You ugly as shit, Yo!"

"And you are fine?" I replied as he drove off.

At one point in my life, I would have gone home and cried and prayed for lighter skin, longer hair, and a smaller frame. The next day, I would have gotten my hair done in some popular style and would have bought a new outfit that would make me look "cute"... all because of this man's perception of me: as "Ugly."

I had two options at the point of insult: accept it or reject it. Although I was offended that he would say something mean without warrant, I chose the latter. I did not give him the power to validate my beauty.

Who defined you in your life? Did your mother call you fat when you were a kid? Did your brother say that you had big feet? Did your dad call you stupid? Who defines you now?

We often take on other people's definition of us and believe them wholeheartedly. We believe them as if their words are gold.

We must dispose the negativity and honor the positive through affirmations and personal praise. You may have heard years of insults and put-downs from family, lovers and friends. At some point you may have taken their suggestions and made them true for yourself.

What did they say?

1. Mom:

_____
_____
_____
_____
_____
_____
_____
_____

2. Dad:

_____
_____
_____
_____
_____
_____
_____
_____

3. Brother:

_____
_____
_____
_____
_____
_____
_____
_____

4. Sister:

_____
_____
_____
_____
_____
_____
_____
_____
_____

5. Lover:

_____
_____
_____
_____
_____
_____
_____
_____
_____

6. Teacher:

_____
_____
_____
_____
_____
_____
_____
_____
_____

7. Other:

_____
_____
_____
_____
_____
_____
_____
_____
_____

Did you believe it? If so, why?

_____
_____
_____
_____
_____
_____
_____
_____

Who are you? Describe yourself with as many positives as you'd like.

_____
_____
_____
_____
_____
_____
_____
_____

Celebrate HER Now!

Define your excellence and practice it everyday. Excellence is not perfection. What are people allowed to do and not allowed to do or say to you? Boundaries are imperative – people must not be able to run all up in your life and take over. There should be consequences for those who cross your boundaries once you have established them.

Invite quality in your life, when you choose people, places and things. Kick MEDIOCRITY out the door. It's not welcome any more. Understand that you are awesomely human– give perfection the boot!

Some of us live our lives in the past, regretful that things didn't turn out like we had planned or hoped. You are meant to walk the path you are on. It is for you to obtain information on your life's purpose. There are no mistakes or coincidences. I heard a really awesome quote in a good movie called *Thirteen Conversations about One Thing*: *"Life makes sense in reverse."* If you can come to accept this, then all will be well.

Learning to say "NO!"

A **standard** is an established rule of quality and or value.
A **boundary** is a limit, where you would draw the line.

Standard: Honesty is my #1 priority. Dishonesty of any kind has no place in my life.

Boundary: If I am lied to or stolen from, I will question the doer to find out why. If it happens again, I will disassociate myself from this person in my life. I know that I deserve truth and honesty.

Standard: I will only allow people to call me by my name.

Asserting your boundaries: "Will you please stop calling me 'baby', 'boo', 'sweetheart'. It makes me feel uncomfortable. It

113

would make me feel respected and appreciated if you could call me by my name. Thank you."

Standard: I will not have sex with anyone who is under the influence of drugs or alcohol. This includes my spouse.

Boundary: I will physically separate myself from those who are under the influence. Either they will leave or I will go because I know I deserve 100% attention.

Please know that creating standards and asserting boundaries is not an easy process. Be patient but firm. The mission in asserting boundaries is to be at peace with yourself. Be willing to let go of people in your life who cannot respect your boundaries. Many people will take offense to your request, but remember the end result is to maintain a quality of life that works for you. **Choose you.**

Write out your **Standards** here.

1. _____
2. _____
3. _____
4. _____
5. _____
6. _____
7. _____
8. _____
9. _____
10. _____

Family

Example: I will lend money to those who have paid me on time. My loan limit is $400 per year.

What are your boundaries with your family?

1. _____
2. _____
3. _____
4. _____
5. _____

Relationships

EX: Tuesday is my personal day. I will be left alone to replenish my spirit. I will not allow my partner to woo me into doing a couples activity.

What are your boundaries in your relationship?

1. _____
2. _____
3. _____
4. _____
5. _____

Work

EX: Saturday is my Sabbath. I have made it clear to my supervisor that under no circumstances will I work on this day.

What are your boundaries at work?

1. _____
2. _____
3. _____
4. _____
5. _____

Friendship

EX: I will not allow my friends to call me with gossip and negative comments.

What are your boundaries in friendship?

1. _____
2. _____
3. _____
4. _____
5. _____

How would you define personal excellence?

_____
_____
_____
_____

How would you define perfection?

_____
_____
_____
_____

What is the difference between the two?

_____
_____
_____
_____

Please don't stress yourself trying to be perfect... remember that you *are* awesomely human.

I RECOGNIZE MY DESTRUCTIVE PATTERNS AND SEEK SUPPORT AND HELP FROM THE DIVINE AND MY COMMUNITY.

Notes:

_____

_____

_____

_____

_____

_____

_____

_____

_____

_____

_____

_____

_____

_____

_____

_____

_____

_____

_____

_____

_____

_____

_____

_____

Addictions come in many forms. The *American Heritage Medical Dictionary* defines addiction as a habitual, psychological, and physiological dependence on a substance or practice beyond one's voluntary control. Basically: *any thought, action or pattern that has frequent control over you is an addiction.* Addictions are a way to escape/numb emotions or feelings.

Here is a list of common addictions:

- Sex/Pornography/Masturbation/Prostitution
- Work
- Food
- Alcohol
- Drugs: Prescription and Street
- Love/Romanticism/Relationships
- Gambling
- Nicotine
- Caffeine
- Sugar
- Shopping
- Television
- Religion
- Exercise
- Theft

These are just a few, but mostly all of them have a twelve-step program similar to Alcoholic's Anonymous®.

When we use any of the above to avoid dealing with emotional issues in our lives we may be addicted. Some of us are addicted to the concept we call love. In our lack of love or intimacy from our parents in our youth we seek love or the idea of love from others even when they are not worthy of our time.

119

Sometimes we crave attention so badly that we will do anything to get it. Sex is one of the ways women strive for validation. Have you ever heard the quote, *"Men love to get sex and women sex to get love?"* Does this apply to you? We may meet someone on the subway or in the grocery store and take him or her home and give him or her the time of their life, and then create the fantasy that they will be the one because you two are so sexually compatible. Afterwards, we wonder why they don't call us back. We have anal sex when we really don't want it or we think our vaginas belong to whoever is in it at the time.

Relationships
(check all that apply)

- ❏ Do you lose yourself in a relationship and don't come up for air until it's over?
- ❏ Do you feel empty without a mate?
- ❏ What is the role of the opposite/same sex in your life?
- ❏ Where do you think that role comes from?
- ❏ What is the meaning of marriage to you?
- ❏ Are your relationships for you or for your family, co-workers, or friends?
- ❏ Is there more drama and stress than peace and love when it comes to your love life?

Relationships are dangerous for you when you say things like, "I love you more than I love myself," or "I am nothing without you." If you are looking for a superhero to rescue you from your emotional problems or be a superhero to rescue someone else from their problems, you are heading in the direction of self-destruction.

The age-old adage states, *"If you truly love something let it go and if it is to be it will come back to you."* Can you grasp that concept or does this frighten you? Fantasies can be addictive. Sometimes we fantasize about who the person could be or who s/he used to be instead of who s/he is right now.

Hook and Bait

Let's say we have what we consider "big feet." A person comes along, sensing your insecurities about your feet, and begins to admire and acknowledge your feet. S/he may say things like, "Your feet are sooo sexy" or "I can eat off of your feet" or they might even massage your feet or buy you sandals to expose your toes.

Now, you are developing feelings for this person because for the first time in your life, someone has celebrated a part of you that has been a source of shame and hate for so long. You start getting comfortable in this relationship because s/he begins to sing your feet's praises. You start celebrating this person in return because you begin to feel so good about your feet. You start buying things to help them out: cell phones, paying rent, letting them hold your car. After two months, the foot massages have stopped, but six months into the relationships you are still buying and doing stuff for your partner. You justify that the foot massages have stopped because of the stress at work. A year later, you are so deep in love and have invested more and more into this other person, but you begin to feel depleted, used etc.

What this person has done is called hook and bait, just as a worm is the bait for an unsuspecting and hungry fish. You and your insecurities are the bait for those who are leeches, manipulators, and are also very insecure themselves.

Those who are pros at this can smell insecurities, vulnerabilities, and desperation. They play on it. They look for a way to get in, and woo us just enough to get us wide open. In your fantasy you thought the foot worshipping would last forever. They did enough to have you eating out of the palms of their hands.

Is this one of your patterns? If so, celebrate you and love your own feet.

Signs of Addiction:

1. If you find yourself feeling unloved, unwanted and unattractive and you dress very provocatively to hunt for a one night stand at the night club or bar of your choice to remedy the above, then you may be addicted to sex or what you think is love.

2. When you get into an argument with your mate and find yourself reaching in the fridge for chocolate cake or fried chicken to calm yourself down or soothe your emotional wounds, then you may be addicted to food.

3. When you are disregarded or rejected by someone you meet in a social scene and find yourself shopping for a new pair of shoes to make yourself feel better... You may be addicted to shopping.

What kinds of patterns repeat themselves in your life?

_____
_____
_____
_____
_____

Celebrate HER Now!

When do you eat, have sex, enter into a relationship, smoke cigarettes, shop, gamble, drink, watch pornography, masturbate and why?

_____
_____
_____
_____
_____
_____
_____
_____

Define love:

_____
_____
_____
_____
_____
_____
_____
_____
_____
_____
_____
_____
_____
_____
_____
_____
_____
_____
_____
_____
_____

What is the difference between love and sex?

_____
_____
_____
_____
_____
_____
_____
_____
_____
_____
_____
_____
_____
_____
_____
_____
_____
_____
_____
_____
_____
_____
_____
_____
_____
_____
_____
_____
_____
_____

I AM AWARE OF HOW SEXISM AND RACISM AFFECTS ME!

Notes:

_____

_____

_____

_____

_____

_____

_____

_____

_____

_____

_____

_____

_____

_____

_____

_____

_____

_____

_____

_____

_____

_____

_____

_____

_____

Just as racism and classism create a value judgment of superiority/inferiority based on skin color, other physical characteristics and material wealth, sexism creates a judgment or set of standards based on the gender of a human being.

Media Messages

Analyze your favorite African-American TV show and compare your findings with those of a "Caucasian show" and write down your feelings about the characters actions. Pay attention to the roles of women in each of the shows.

TV show #1 _____

TV show #2 _____

1) Who gets the laughs and why? Please describe the character.

_____
_____
_____
_____

2) Do you think these scenarios are realistic?

_____
_____
_____
_____

3) What are your thoughts as you watch this show?

_____
_____
_____
_____

4) Which characters would you like to befriend or date? Why?

_____
_____
_____
_____

5) What is the difference between the roles of women and men in the shows?

_____
_____
_____
_____

6) What jobs do they have?

_____
_____
_____
_____

7) How often do the women talk and what do they talk about?

_____
_____
_____
_____

8) What compliments or put-downs do they get? Does it have anything to do with complexion?

_____
_____
_____
_____

9) Who is desirable? What are their physical characteristics?

_____

_____

_____

_____

10) Are pregnant women visible? What is being said about pregnancy?

_____

_____

_____

_____

11) Do you notice any difference between the wants and needs of the male and female characters in the show? What are the differences and why?

_____

_____

_____

_____

12) How is this show different from those needs of females and males in "Caucasian shows"?

_____

_____

_____

_____

13) What do you think of your findings?

_____

_____

_____

_____

14) Are older women portrayed as attractive? Are they respected? Valued for their wisdom?

_____

_____

_____

_____

15) Who is more concerned with their physical appearance? Why do you think they are?

_____

_____

_____

_____

16) Do dark skin women deserve love?

_____

_____

_____

_____

17) Do heavier women deserve love?

_____

_____

_____

_____

18) How are you similar to your findings? How are you different?

_____

_____

_____

_____

Music has always embodied subtle but persistent sexist lyrics. Whether sung by a woman or man, the usual message is that women are to serve, please, and receive whatever is presented to them and honor the wants, desires and fantasies of men above themselves and their needs. Whether it is Major Harris and Luther Vandross justifying rape in very seductive ways in the song *Love Won't Let Me Wait,*

"And I refuse to leave till I see the mornin' sun
Because love won't let me wait
Not another minute

Ooh...ooh...ooh...yeah...yeah...

And I won't take the blame
That love won't let me wait." [13]

Or, R. Kelly comparing women to cars in both his songs *You Remind Me of Something* and *Ignition:*

"You remind me of my jeep, I wanna ride it
Something like my sound, I wanna pump it
Girl you look just like my cars, I wanna wax it
And something like my bank account
I wanna spend it, baby"

"No more hopin' and wishin'
I'm about to take my key 'n'
Stick it in da ignition." [14]

Or Destiny's Child promising superhuman and fantastic desires in Cater 2 U:

Remain the same chick you fell in love with.
I'll keep it tight, I'll keep my figure right
I'll keep my hair fixed…
When you come home late tap me on my shoulder, I'll roll over
Baby I heard you, I'm here to serve you
I want to give you my breath, my strength, my will to be here
That's the least I can do,
Let me cater to you" [15]

Sexism is everywhere. It is part of the American way. Messages like these devalue the greatness of womanhood and leaves little to no room for her wants and needs beyond sex and servitude.

How are these lyrics sexist?

_____
_____
_____

What other sexist lyrics have affected your outlook on life?

_____
_____
_____

Self-Work: Begin listening to some of your favorite songs. What are the men saying and what do they want? What are the women saying and what do they want? How does this affect the roles and self-definition of the women that you know? Does art imitate life or does life imitate art?

I ACKNOWLEDGE
HOW I FEEL.

Lacey C. Clark!

Notes:

_____
_____
_____
_____
_____
_____
_____
_____
_____
_____
_____
_____
_____
_____
_____
_____
_____
_____
_____
_____
_____
_____
_____
_____
_____
_____
_____

Have you ever tried to make excuses for how you felt? Did you know something was wrong but because you didn't want to make a fuss, you kept your mouth shut and said nothing until you've blown spilled milk totally out of proportion?

Many times we get really angry with the person who stepped on our foot but in actuality we are angry at ourselves. We may be angry about our relationship, job, family life, financial situation or progress in life, but instead of taking responsibility for how we feel about ourselves, we lash out at everyone else. We blame the mail carrier for coming too late or we curse out the waitress at the restaurant for bringing us Ginger Ale instead of Sprite, but deep down inside we know that it has nothing to with these people. These reactions are only symptoms of deeper "dis-ease" of us not dealing with a larger problem and taking our issues out on others.

Do you know how to speak the feeling language?

Feeling Language 101

Circle words that you have used to describe your feelings. Use a dictionary to look up the definitions for those words that are foreign to you.

Open	Happy	Alive	Good
understanding	great	playful	calm
confident	gay	courageous	peaceful
reliable	joyous	energetic	at ease
easy	lucky	liberated	comfort
amazed	fortunate	optimistic	pleased
free	delighted	provocative	encouraged
sympathetic	overjoyed	impulsive	clever
interested	gleeful	free	surprised
satisfied	thankful	frisky	content
receptive	important	animated	quiet
accepting	festive	spirited	certain
kind	ecstatic	thrilled	relaxed

Love	Interested	Positive	Strong
loving	concerned	eager	impulsive
considerate	affected	keen	free
affectionate	fascinated	earnest	sure
sensitive	intrigued	intent	certain
tender	absorbed	anxious	rebellious
devoted	inquisitive	inspired	unique
attracted	nosy	determined	dynamic
passionate	snoopy	excited	tenacious
admiration	engrossed	enthusiastic	hardy
warm	curious	bold	secure

Angry	Depressed	Confused	Helpless
irritated	lousy	upset	incapable
enraged	disappointed	doubtful	alone
hostile	discouraged	uncertain	paralyzed
insulting	ashamed	indecisive	fatigued
sore	powerless	perplexed	useless
annoyed	diminished	embarrassed	inferior
upset	guilty	hesitant	vulnerable
hateful	dissatisfied	shy	empty
unpleasant	miserable	stupefied	forced
offensive	detestable	disillusioned	hesitant
bitter	repugnant	unbelieving	despair
aggressive	despicable	skeptical	frustrated
resentful	disgusting	distrustful	distressed
inflamed	abominable	misgiving	woeful
provoked	terrible	lost	pathetic
incensed	in despair	unsure	tragic
infuriated	sulky	uneasy	in a stew
crossed	bad	pessimistic	dominated

Indifferent	Afraid	Hurt	Sad
insensitive	fearful	crushed	tearful
dull	terrified	tormented	sorrowful
nonchalant	suspicious	deprived	pained
neutral	anxious	pained	grief
reserved	alarmed	tortured	anguish
weary	panic	dejected	desolate
bored	nervous	rejected	desperate

preoccupied	scared	injured	pessimistic
cold	worried	offended	unhappy
disinterested	frightened	afflicted	lonely
lifeless	timid	aching	grieved

Definitions:

_____

_____

_____

_____

_____

_____

_____

_____

_____

_____

_____

_____

_____

_____

_____

_____

_____

_____

_____

_____

_____

_____

_____

_____

_____

Write a 250-300 word autobiography of a certain era of your life, i.e. high school graduation, birth of first child, your teen years, your 20's or your 30's. Please use at least 25 different feeling words to describe this era.

_____
_____
_____
_____
_____
_____
_____
_____

Self-Work:

> For one week, practice telling the people in your immediate circle how you feel. Remember, those you communicate with are not responsible for making you feel better or worse. Simply share how you feel and begin asking yourself "Why? Why do I feel this way?" Once you get the hang of it, keep going. The answer is always within you.

> Observe conversations that you are not a part of throughout the day, specifically between those who are closest to you. Have they expressed their feelings?

PERSONAL REVIEW

Now that you have assessed your greatness and your areas of improvement, why do you love you?

Please write a love letter to yourself explaining why you are important to you. Be sure to include your self-discoveries and go on and on about what makes you special. Remember, this is for you and not to impress anyone else.

Dear _____,

I love you because

_____

_____

_____

_____

_____

_____

_____

_____

_____

_____

_____

_____

_____

_____

_____

_____

_____

_____

_____

_____

Lacey C. Clark!

_____
_____
_____
_____
_____
_____
_____
_____
_____
_____
_____
_____
_____
_____
_____
_____
_____
_____
_____
_____
_____
_____
_____
_____
_____
_____
_____

Signed,

_____

SELF-LOVE ACTION GOALS:

Now that you have completed this section of the book...

What are your self-love action goals?

Sample Goal: I will create a mental health/self-love day every week. It will be just for me.

Action steps:

1. Create a self-love budget.
2. Record dates in my calendar so I can begin preparation.
3. Make reservations for lunch/dinner/spa for three months.
4. Alert all of my close family members of the times and dates of my special day.
5. Make a list of all the activities I aspire to do for me or with me.

Goal #1

_____
_____
_____

Action Steps

1. _____
2. _____
3. _____
4. _____
5. _____

Goal #2

_____
_____
_____

Action Steps

    1. _____
    2. _____
    3. _____
    4. _____
    5. _____

Goal #3

_____
_____
_____

Action Steps

    1. _____
    2. _____
    3. _____
    4. _____
    5. _____

Goal #4

_____
_____
_____

Action Steps

1. _____
2. _____
3. _____
4. _____
5. _____

Goal #5

_____

_____

_____

Action Steps

1. _____
2. _____
3. _____
4. _____
5. _____

Lacey C. Clark!

MISSION 11

I EMBRACE OUR FEMALE YOUTH BY . . .

Lacey C. Clark!

BEING AN EXAMPLE!

Lacey C. Clark!

Notes:

_____
_____
_____
_____
_____
_____
_____
_____
_____
_____
_____
_____
_____
_____
_____
_____
_____
_____
_____
_____
_____
_____
_____

Celebrate HER Now!

Lead by example - give *HER* a model to aspire to. What kind of example are you? Place a picture of yourself here:

My picture here!

What do you have to offer?

_____
_____
_____
_____
_____
_____
_____
_____
_____
_____
_____
_____
_____
_____
_____
_____
_____
_____
_____
_____
_____
_____
_____
_____
_____
_____
_____

MAKING A FINANCIAL INVESTMENT IN *HER* WELL BEING.

Notes:

_____

_____

_____

_____

_____

_____

_____

_____

_____

_____

_____

_____

_____

_____

_____

_____

_____

_____

_____

_____

_____

_____

Spending Diary

What are you spending your money on? Is it possible for you to set aside $10-200 a month in an investment fund for *HER* educational, personal, financial or emotional well-being? If you smoke, could you cut back on the extra pack of cigarettes per week? If you eat out everyday, can you pack your lunch instead? The money saved can be used for a college fund, housing allowance, traveling fund, etc. Invest time and money in *HER* well-being. Could you cut back on expenses to cut back on hours at work to invest in *HER*?

What expenses could you cut back on?

Reduced Expense	Money Saved	Money Allocated

Allocation Options:

- Education Savings Account College
- 529 College Savings Plan
- Custodial Account for traveling, camps, etc.
- Self-Awareness Account for books and nurturing activities

There should be restrictions on *HER* access to the funding. She may want to tap into it for a pair of jeans and/or for concert tickets. The account should remain for its original purpose until she is mature enough to make responsible choices about what to do with it.

UNDERSTANDING THAT I DO NOT KNOW EVERYTHING!!!

Lacey C. Clark!

Notes:

_____
_____
_____
_____
_____
_____
_____
_____
_____
_____
_____
_____
_____
_____
_____
_____
_____
_____
_____
_____
_____
_____
_____
_____

Listen to *HER* without quickly responding. Breathe. Think. Digest. Respond. Refrain from reacting. Put yourself in *HER* shoes. Remember you were a teenager at one point and someone older that you didn't agree with your actions, decisions, and choices. We have often judged teenagers for having risky behavior or for "pushing the envelope" by saying or doing too much. What were you doing at *HER* age? What were our closest friends doing? Sometimes we forget that we used to sneak out of the house, flash boys our panties, or get our "freak on" in and after school. Admit this to yourself. Admit it to *HER*.

What kind of risqué things did you do as a teenager?

_____
_____
_____
_____
_____
_____
_____
_____
_____
_____

How can you compare some of your old behavior to the behavior of the young girls today?

_____
_____
_____
_____
_____
_____
_____
_____
_____

Make a conscious effort not to degrade or devalue *HER* thinking. You may explain how something else may be valuable to you and why.

Watch judgmental words and phrases like, "you need to," "you betta," "you gotta" or words that belittle her value *like silly, retarded, idiotic, stupid, ridiculous* and replace them with words to make *HER* reach further.

"You" statements are accusatory. How do you feel when people point the finger at you? Nine times out of ten your answer would be not good, right? So, refrain from using them when trying to communicate something you disagree with. Respond with, "Interesting, I would have to see that developed further, etc..." instead of "You are not thinking."

Instead of:

"You need to take that skirt off. It's too tight!" Try to rephrase with a question. This makes *HER* think and helps *HER* take responsibility for *HER* actions.

Example: "Do you believe that your body is precious and sacred? Do you think you are conveying respect, dignity, and inner beauty with what you are wearing? How can we re-do this outfit so that it says 'I am worthy of respect'?"

Instead of:

You are acting like a little whore!
Try: "Show them what you have beyond your body! What do you have to offer?"

Practice rephrasing your words. What have you said that you could have rephrased:

_____

_____

_____

_____

How could you have rephrased it?

_____

_____

_____

_____

_____

DELEGATING AUTHORITY.

Notes:

_____

_____

_____

_____

_____

_____

_____

_____

_____

_____

_____

_____

_____

_____

_____

_____

_____

_____

_____

_____

_____

_____

_____

Do not be afraid to delegate difficult situations to a responsible person that she deems hip or cool.

She is who she is. Your job is to show *HER* healthier options and choices. Certain areas may not be your strong points, but that does not mean that they should not be addressed. Seek out someone that you trust or a trusted source of good information that you can send *HER* to for direction; your sister, your best friends, niece, her doctor, etc.

What are some issues that you have been having problems with in the past?

_____
_____
_____
_____
_____
_____
_____
_____
_____
_____

Who can you identify as your support team to help you through the difficult times?

_____
_____
_____
_____
_____
_____
_____
_____
_____

Lacey C. Clark!

WANTING TO KNOW ABOUT *HER*.

Notes:

_____
_____
_____
_____
_____
_____
_____
_____
_____
_____
_____
_____
_____
_____
_____
_____
_____
_____
_____
_____
_____
_____
_____
_____

Celebrate HER Now!

Ask questions that encourage *HER* to talk about *HER*self:

- ◇ How was your day in school?
- ◇ What are you thankful for today?
- ◇ What do you think of the (relevant source in the media)?
- ◇ What are you doing this weekend?
- ◇ What are your summer plans?
- ◇ How is the situation with _____ going?
- ◇ Tell me what you like about your favorite song.
- ◇ What did you think of the scene where _____ did_____to _____, could you see yourself doing that? Why?
- ◇ Do you think xyz is attractive? Why?
- ◇ What made you want to get that tattoo?
- ◇ Where do you see yourself in 5, 10, 15 years?
- ◇ Do you want children?
- ◇ How will you raise your children?

Caution:

1. When asking honest, real questions, be prepared to get honest, real answers. She might tell you something you do not expect to hear. For example, she may identify *HER*self as a lesbian or girl who likes girls. This may or may not be a phase. Please do not try and beat, judge or criticize *HER*. This will only drive you two apart. You might be the only person that she has who will listen. If you feel that you cannot be open to how she feels about *HER*self, seek out someone who is more open. Don't leave *HER* to the wolves because you don't agree with *HER*.

I had a 15-year-old student in my Self-love 101 class who identified as a lesbian. She stated that *HER* mother would frequently pressure *HER* and try to arrange meetings with boys for *HER* to "get some dick." She was 15. This was the mother's way to try to "remedy" *HER* daughter's "problem." Was this appropriate?

2. Be aware, some youth may take your question asking as probing. If you are the parent, you have a right to know what is going on in your child's life. If you are a (wo)mentor (aunt, teacher, older friend, etc.) only ask when appropriate.

Let *HER* speak *HER* language… listen to *HER* passion… *HER* emotions. Remember this is about allowing *HER* to develop *HER* greatness. It's, not about you judging how she talks. Look past the slang and reach for the emotion. But, gently, coach *HER* to speak with clearer diction and grammar.

Get hip on the slang so you can communicate or at least understand *HER* without stopping *HER* every five minutes. There are always a few new words for good, bad, excited, such as "off da hook", "dope", "fresh," "whack," "bangin'," etc.

What is the current lingo? Make your own "slangtionary" here:

Good:

_____

_____

_____

_____

Bad:

_____

_____

_____

_____

Clothes:

_____
_____
_____
_____

Shoes:

_____
_____
_____
_____

Dancing really well:

_____
_____
_____
_____

Car:

_____
_____
_____
_____

House:

_____
_____
_____
_____

Drugs:

_____
_____
_____
_____

Sex:

_____

_____

_____

_____

Practice your newly learned slang in the mirror. If you don't get it quite right when you are around *HER*, she can at least chuckle at the attempt. Do you remember how you felt when a teacher or parent tried to speak your "Slanguage"? It might have made you feel a bit more comfortable to know they were trying to relate to you. It may come out "corny," but have fun and laugh at yourself.

Engage in media exchanges. Give *HER* an opportunity to share *HER* music and the media she loves. Actively listen to and watch it with openness. Scan for things that relate to your era. Share your era with *HER*. But remember, ol' school ain't new school- your way of thinking is not *HER* way of thinking.

Although some experiences may relate to or be complimentary to yours, please know that the way you grew up is different from what she is experiencing now. Refrain from comparing your day to the "good old days" as if *HER*s are the "bad new days." Listen more than you speak.

Help *HER* talk about intimate body parts with you. Use *HER* media and music as catalysts for difficult conversations about sex, pregnancy, vagina and relationships. These are also known as teaching opportunities. You could use a scene from John Singleton's movie "Baby Boy" [16] to talk about how sex is used to control or remedy emotional problems.

Explain that *HER* body has a functional, spiritual purpose beyond pleasure and carnal excitement.

PRAISING *HER*!

Notes:

_____
_____
_____
_____
_____
_____
_____
_____
_____
_____
_____
_____
_____
_____
_____
_____
_____
_____
_____
_____
_____
_____
_____
_____
_____
_____

Call *HER* beautiful!
Buy *HER* flowers.
Give *HER* as much positive energy and goodness as possible.

What can you say that would make *HER* feel beautiful, good, and celebrated?

_____
_____
_____
_____
_____

Compliment people, especially other women, when you are in *HER* presence. Please be genuine. Giving positive energy to others invites positivity.

Practice here:

_____
_____
_____
_____
_____

Lacey C. Clark!

ASSISTING IN MOLDING *HER* EXCELLENCE.

Notes:

_____
_____
_____
_____
_____
_____
_____
_____
_____
_____
_____
_____
_____
_____
_____
_____
_____
_____
_____
_____
_____
_____
_____
_____

Encourage *HER* to define *HER* excellence and *HER* standards. Hold *HER* accountable. If she says she is going to meet you at 3:30 pm, and she shows at 3:35 pm without calling, mention it to *HER*. Explain that 3:35, although arriving only five minutes late is still late and that a standard of excellence is arriving 10 minutes early. She needs to get it now, for she will be joining the workforce someday.

Encourage *HER* to keep a day planner as a way to keep track of time and *HER* goals. Everyday, she should be working toward a tangible goal for school, college, travel, enrichment, etc.

What goals has she set for any of the above?

_____

_____

_____

_____

_____

_____

_____

_____

_____

What is *HER* plan to make *HER* goals a reality?

_____

_____

_____

_____

_____

_____

_____

_____

_____

_____

Please know that she is competing to fit in with *HER* peers. Peer pressure is a "motha", especially if she is a follower. Think back to when you were in school and how you might have wanted to fit in with your friends. One develops leadership by being in positive leadership roles. Find opportunities to make *HER* a leader and hold *HER* accountable. For example, put *HER* in charge of planning and structuring your quality time with each other. Tell *HER* to plan a special celebration day for you both (Perhaps on National Self-love Day, www.sisterssanctuary.org).

Give *HER* the budget and tell *HER* the sky is the limit. Give *HER* boundaries and coach her to create standards. Planning a "girl's day" will allow you to see and meet *HER* friends. This may also be an opportunity to positively influence *HER* circle of friends as well.

How else can you increase *HER* leadership capacity?

_____
_____
_____
_____
_____
_____
_____
_____
_____
_____
_____
_____
_____
_____
_____
_____

SUPPORTING *HER* IN BUILDING *HER* SACRED SPACE.

Notes:

_____

_____

_____

_____

_____

_____

_____

_____

_____

_____

_____

_____

_____

_____

_____

_____

_____

_____

_____

_____

_____

_____

_____

Help *HER* to set up or maintain a sacred space that speaks to *HER* inner-self. She may want to hang pictures of chart-topping celebrities. While this is okay, help *HER* to see other ways to decorate for *HER* positive affirmation, i.e. using colors, words and posters that empower *HER*. If she doesn't have a room of *HER* own, perhaps she can find a corner or place where she can erect a portable sacred space or maybe you can help *HER* with a poster she can hang up if she shares a room with someone else.

What does she like? Can you bring *HER* anything that may compliment *HER* space?

_____
_____
_____
_____
_____
_____
_____
_____
_____
_____
_____
_____
_____
_____
_____
_____
_____
_____

Lacey C. Clark!

ASSISTING *HER* IN MAKING A SPIRITUAL INVESTMENT IN OTHERS.

Lacey C. Clark!

Notes:

_____
_____
_____
_____
_____
_____
_____
_____
_____
_____
_____
_____
_____
_____
_____
_____
_____
_____
_____
_____
_____
_____
_____

Encourage *HER* to invest in the intangible by volunteering for humanity. If she loves to do hair perhaps she can wash hair for the elderly at a hospice or seniors home. If she enjoys writing poetry she can channel *HER* energy in doing a poetry reading for *HER* church or community center. Homeless shelters always need help. Find volunteer opportunities that support what she likes to do. Go with *HER* and help *HER* if need be. She can get some practical experience by helping others. She will gain a sense of importance and build *HER* own self-esteem by giving back. This will allow *HER* to appreciate *HER* own blessings.

List possibilities here:

What she likes to do:	Opportunities

Lacey C. Clark!

BEING OPEN MINDED!

Notes:

_____
_____
_____
_____
_____
_____
_____
_____
_____
_____
_____
_____
_____
_____
_____
_____
_____
_____
_____
_____
_____
_____
_____
_____
_____
_____

Stay open minded. Our youth are growing up much faster than we did. You might be surprised by what they know how to do, and can probably do better than you. They have access to more, they see more, and do more. This may or may not be in *HER* favor. Be open-minded about what she has to share. Ask questions and research what you don't understand.

What did you find out from our youth that you didn't know?

_____

_____

_____

_____

Lacey C. Clark!

PRACTICING FORGIVENESS.

Lacey C. Clark!

Notes:

_____
_____
_____
_____
_____
_____
_____
_____
_____
_____
_____
_____
_____
_____
_____
_____
_____
_____
_____
_____
_____
_____
_____
_____
_____
_____
_____

You both will have challenges. Please remember it is not about what happens to you, but how you react to what happens to you. Things will happen, but it's imperative to have the tools to manage what happens. This interactive guide is your beginning.

Stay consistent and stay present. You need you; she needs you. Remember to assert your boundaries, and be firm but loving... explain why you have them.

How have you practiced forgiveness?

_____
_____
_____
_____
_____
_____
_____
_____

What are some of the benefits of forgiveness?

_____
_____
_____
_____
_____
_____
_____

Lacey C. Clark!

12 - Month Action Plan

The intention of this action plan is to have you spend at least 5 hours of quality time with the youth per month. An example could be 3 hours at the movies or at a volunteer opportunity, a one hour lunch, and a one hour phone conversation.

This plan is designed to gradually build a relationship with someone that you do not know. If the youth is someone in your circle like your daughter, niece or cousin some suggestions may still apply. Be patient and take it one step at a time.

Month #1
Identify youth to support:

- Contact an organization like *Big Brother, Big Sister*.
- Reach out to a family member you haven't seen recently.
- Ask your Community Center about mentoring possibilities.

Action Taken:

_____
_____
_____
_____

Month #2
Block out time to prepare your finances to support the youth. What expenses will you cut back on?

Action Taken:

_____
_____
_____
_____

Month # 3

Make contact. Set-up a date at a public location something not too intimate and very casual, i.e. a bowling alley, arcade, poetry reading, etc, whatever she likes. If she doesn't know what she likes, expose *HER* to something to see what she thinks.

Action Taken:

_____

_____

_____

_____

Month #4

Support something she does. If she is having an event of some kind or working on a project, can you lend a helping hand?

Action Taken:

_____

_____

_____

_____

Month #5

Invite *HER* to lunch at an upscale restaurant. Be sure that it is not too sophisticated. Ask *HER* to wear something professionally casual. You may want to coach *HER* in *HER* clothing choice.

Action Taken:

_____

_____

_____

_____

Month #6

Take *HER* to an event that will benefit *HER* education. Go to the library and research powerful women of the past and present i.e., Harriet Tubman, Sojourner Truth, Zora Neal Hurston, Ethel Waters, Bessie Smith, Ntozake Shange, Susan Lori Parks, Queen Nefertari, Hatshepsut and Makeda. This may help *HER* to understand that women are more than just video hoes and sex objects.

Action Taken:

_____

_____

_____

_____

_____

Month #7

Create a task for something outdoors i.e. swimming, beach, hiking, kayaking, walk-a-thon, run-a-thon, etc.

Action Taken:

_____

_____

_____

_____

Month #8

A day in the life of you, *HER* mother, mentor. Show *HER* your daily activities.

Action Taken:

_____

_____

_____

_____

Month# 9

Have *HER* plan a day of activities for just the two of you. Tell *HER* your budget. See to it that she makes it happen, but let *HER* make mistakes. If she plans a picnic and forgets the bread, just eat the lunchmeat alone.

Action Taken:

_____

_____

_____

_____

Month # 10

Help with a project. If she doesn't have one maybe you can create one together! Try interesting *HER* in entrepreneurship or fundraising for something that she really wants, but does not have the money to buy. Show *HER* how to "use what you got to get what you want."

Action Taken:

_____

_____

_____

_____

Month#11

Plan a day trip to somewhere fun and adventurous like a festival, amusement park, Caribbean Carnival (in your closest city), or white water rafting.

Action Taken:

_____

_____

_____

_____

Month#12

Yeaaaaaaaaah! You completed a year of investing in the mental, physical, emotional, and financial well being of female youth. Keep Going! She still needs you. You still need you.

Action Taken:

_____
_____
_____
_____

For more ideas check out: www.sisterssanctuary.org

Lacey C. Clark!

Glossary

Affirmations - Something declared to be true. A positive statement or judgment.

Custodial Account - An account created at a bank, brokerage firm or mutual fund company that is managed by an adult for a minor that is under the age of 18 to 21 (depending on state legislation).

Exploitation - An act that exploits or victimizes someone (treats them unfairly)

Imperialism - A policy of extending your rule over foreign countries, or any instance of aggressive extension of authority

Meditation - To train, calm, or empty the mind, often by achieving an altered state, as by focusing on a single object or concept.

Mentee - One who is mentored.

Mentor - To serve as a trusted counselor or teacher to (another person).

Middle Passage - the journey of slave trading ships from the west coast of Africa, where Africans were obtained, across the Atlantic, and sold or, in some cases, traded for goods such as molasses, which was used in the making of rum. Packed like sardines, below deck in filthy conditions that brought about infectious disease and death, at least 1 million Africans lost their lives. The ships would travel east to west across the Atlantic on a voyage lasting at least five weeks, and sometimes as long as three months

Patriarchy - A social system in which the father is the head of the family and men have authority over women and children.

Sacred - Worthy of respect or dedication. Highly valued.

Sanctuary - A sacred place, a place of refuge.

Self-Work - An activity designed or created to develop a deeper sense of self-awareness. Often used within a *Sisters' Sanctuary^{TM}* session. Used in lieu of "homework".

Sexism - Attitudes, conditions, or behaviors that promote stereotyping of social roles based on gender, especially discrimination against women

Tofu - A protein-rich food coagulated from an extract of soybeans and used in salads and various cooked foods.

Sister Science
(AKA FUN FACTS ABOUT WOMEN)

1. Men have nipples because in the womb the fetus develops for the first few weeks as a female. After about eight weeks the male genes on the Y chromosome kick in and begin to change the fetus into a male: changing the development of the genitals.

2. A penis is an over developed clitoris.

3. The navel is a reminder that all human beings come from the womb of woman.

4. Women who live to together often menstruate together. This phenomenon is called Menstrual Synchrony.

Lacey C. Clark!

References

1. Sjoo, Monica and Mor, Barbara. *Great Cosmic Mother*, Harper San Francisco, 1991.
2. Sjoo, Monica and Mor, Barbara. *Great Cosmic Mother*, Harper San Francisco, 1991.
3. Notorious B.I.G., <u>Big Poppa</u>, Bad Boy, 2000.
4. Lil Jon & The East Side Boyz, <u>Get Low</u>, BME/TVT (2005)
5. Scott, Jill, <u>The Thickness</u>, Hidden Beach (2000)
6. Akinyele, <u>Put It In Your Mouth</u>, Volcano (1996)
7. Bravehearts featuring NAS, <u>Oochie Wally</u>, Sony (2000)
8. Nelly, <u>Flap Your Wings</u>, Universal (2004)
9. Dr. Afrika, Laila, *African Holistic Health*, A&B Publishers Group, 2004.
10. Making The Grade On Women's Health: A National and State-by-State Report Card:" (Washington: National Women's Law Center, August 2000)
11. Robertson, Robin, *"366 Simply Delicious Dairy Free Recipes"*, from Black Vegetarians.Org (2005)
12. Bolles, Richard N., "What Color is Your Parachute?"(2003)
13. Harris, Major, <u>Love Won't Let Me Wait</u> , Hot Productions (1976)
14. Kelly, R., <u>You Remind Me Of Something</u>, Jive (1995)
15. Destiny's Child, <u>Cater 2 U</u>, Columbia/Sony (2004)
16. Singleton, John, *Baby Boy*, Columbia Pictures (2001)

* The Memory Net process was taught to me by Udda Bartholomew; Vocational Liberation. (Pg. 70)

Lacey C. Clark!

Celebrate HER Now!

Acknowledgements

Tha Motha, Denise L. Clark; Ronald E. Clark Sr. Ronald Clark Jr.; Karen Taylor Bass; Andrew Morrison; Tia D. Smith; Nikki Powerhouse; St. Clair Alphonso Brown; Abhita Austin; My Clark Family; My Broadus Family; My Smallwood Family; My NYU family, Brother Yumy Odom/PASCEP, Reuben Jones/Frontline Dads; Abdullah Bey; Angela Cunningham; Marcia Lyssy, Darlene Attah, Eustace Kangaju, Faye Fitz, Varma Mitchell, Cherrill Wilson, Andrea C. Voight, Tim Bennett, Carolyn Delaurentis, Carol Hendrix, Steve Williams/Small Business Development Center at Temple University; School District of Philadelphia/Horace Arthur Trent III; The Philadelphia High School for Creative and Performing Arts/Elsa Johnson Bass, Mel Williams, Johnny C. Whaley Jr., Stacy Redmond, Class of 1996; All the supportive school Principals of the *Sisters' Sanctuary Self-love 101 Curriculum*;

Nana; Ra'chelle Rogers; Aisha Winfield/AIB Marketing; Jill Scott, Blues Babe Foundation; Syretta Scott/Duafe; The New Freedom Theater/John E Allen Jr., My Teachers and demonstrators, Nieka Wanya Brown, Sadequa Murray, Nya Joy Payton-RIP; Iola Carter, Rebecca Clayton; Ohemah Konadu-Addai; Fatimaah Gamble, Toni C. Mack; Antar Bush; Steven Thornton; Judy Burke; Jennifer Adamek; All students of Sisters' Sanctuary, The first set of Sisters' Sanctuary members, My sisterfriends from Ghana, Noro, Octavia, Alesia, Keyshanda –RIP.

My Girls from around tha' Way- Chanel, Danielle, Chaundria, Veda, Robin, Le-Le, Tammy-RIP, Tiffany, Khadijah, Lyric-Cuz ; Boyz in Da hood- Ricky, Rafiq and Terrell. The Strawberry Mansion Section of North Philadelphia.

All of you (and soooo many more) have added to me and my experiences and I thank you.

Lacey C. Clark!

About The Author

Lacey C. Clark! deemed the *"Hip-Hop Oprah Winfrey"* is the Lead Life Coach and founder of *Sisters' Sanctuary*^{TM}.

Raised in North Philadelphia, Ms. Clark! has over 15 years of experience in empowering youth and adults and is happy to share her expertise with the community. She holds a BFA in film and television from New York University, where she was named a Founder's Scholar and recipient of the William H. Cosby Future Filmmakers Award. While at NYU, she founded the *Black Family Reunion* organization, a community service oriented club that gives back to inner-city communities.

Ms. Clark's professional career includes working in the development department of Spike Lee's production company, *40 Acres and a Mule*, and teaching abroad in Ghana West Africa at the *National Film and Television Institute*. She was invited to present on behalf of Sisters' Sanctuary^{TM} at the *World Federation of Mental Health Practitioners* Conference in Melbourne, Australia, February 2003.

Sisters' Sanctuary^{TM} has partnered with Jill Scott's *Blues Babe Foundation* and has been featured in *Rolling Out, The Philadelphia Tribune, The Daily News, The Philadelphia Weekly and Shades of Opinion, Channel 35, WYBE, Philadelphia and BET's show "Remixed"*. Ms. Clark's hobbies include, people watching, spa hopping, and dancing to inspirational house music.

She teaches at the *Pan African Studies Community Education Program* (PASCEP) at Temple University and is a trainer, motivational speaker and lecturer.

Sisters' Sanctuary Services

Sisters' Sanctuary^{TM} offers the following on-site services:

- ***Inner Beau-Tea* Parties**^{TM}

The *Sisters' Sanctuary*^{TM} **Inner Beau-Tea Party** ^{SM} is a real tea party that reinstates the African Proverb, "it takes a village- to- raise- a- child" by providing a non-judgmental space for adult women and female youth within the Hip-Hop generation to exchange points of view on topics such as: Father-daughter dynamics, "Daddy's Little Girl," and "Sexism in the City: How sexism affects Black women." The overall mission of this venture is to encourage adult women to spend 8 hours of quality time with female youth per month and to compliment each other's inner beauty.

- ***Peace-n-Playshops*^{SM}**

These interactive workshops explore themes of self-esteem and empowerment, positive body image, sexism, communication, basic nutrition, hair appreciation, sexuality, healthy relationships, parent/child dynamics, obsession and addiction, pampering, mental wellness and stress reduction.

- **Mini-Retreats** (1day)

Retreats include various wellness topics for developing women, self-message techniques, Intro to forgiveness, stress reduction, Mental Wellness, Body Ownership, creative journaling techniques, pamper planning, Aromatherapy 101, and How to create your own sanctuary on a budget.

- **Staff Training**-How to Reach the Hip-Hop Generation. From Holla'in to Hatin': Decoding Hip-Hop Culture and Communication for the Confused and Frustrated Adult.

Lacey C. Clark!

Sensitivity training for teachers, administrators and parents who interact with the Hip-Hop Generation. Presents techniques on how to communicate effectively for optimal academic and personal performance. Encourages adults to look past the façade and through the language to discover the humanity of young people.

Sensitivity training and empowerment training for teachers, administrators and parents who interact with **female youth** of the Hip - Hop Generation. Exposes techniques on how to improve self-esteem and create a positive and affirming classroom, school or home environment. Encourages adults to inspire female youth to make healthier choices regarding relationships, sex and sexuality, parent/child and alcohol and drugs.

- **Female Sensitivity Training** for Boys and Men.

Interactive workshops for males ages 8 to 108 that teach the spiritual, physical and emotional value of womanhood.

COMING TO A CITY NEAR YOU!

- **Celebrate *HER* Now!** *Self –Lovinar^{SM}* Tour

A two-day seminar that puts self-love and embracing female youth into practice. Seminar topics focus on body image, boundaries and self-dating. Second day includes a multi-generation Inner BeauTea Party ^{SM}.

- You can start a *Sisters' Sanctuary^{TM}* in your community! More information coming soon.

We want to hear from you, visit us online,
www.celebratehernow.com or email us,
youaresacred@sisterSSanctuary.org

<u>Notes:</u>